WRITERS AND THEIR WORK

ISOBEL ARMSTRONG
General Editor

R. K. NARAYAN

T0323839

R. K. NARAYAN

Nicholas Grene

NORTHCOTE

BRITISH
COUNCIL

First published in 2011 by Northcote House Publishers Ltd, Horndon, Tavistock, Devon, PL19 9NQ, United Kingdom.
Tel: +44 (01822) 810066. Fax: +44 (01822) 810034.

British Library Cataloguing-in-Publication Data
A catalogue record for this book is available from the British Library

ISBN 978-0-7463-1078-6 hardcover
ISBN 978-0-7463-0954-4 paperback

Typeset by TW Typesetting, Plymouth, Devon
Printed and bound in the United Kingdom

For Rufus

Contents

Acknowledgements		ix
Biographical Outline		xi
Abbreviations		xv
Introduction		1
1	The Imagination of Malgudi	5
2	Politics and Marriage	35
3	Embedded Myths	56
4	Malgudi and Modernity	83
5	Storytelling Styles	102
Conclusion		120
Notes		124
Bibliography		131
Index		134

Acknowledgements

Grateful acknowledgement is made to the Wallace Literary Agency, Inc. for the Estate of R. K. Narayan for permission to quote from the work of R. K. Narayan: full details are listed below. I am very grateful to Trinity College Dublin for a year's leave of absence in 2008–9 during which this book was written. This also made possible a two month stay in Mysore crucial to its research. I am most grateful for help from colleagues at the University of Mysore including Professor Mahadeva, Drs R. Ramachandra, C. P. Ravichandra and Vijay Seshadri. I benefited greatly from the opportunity to speak with the late T. S. Satyan, and gratefully acknowledge permission to use his wonderful photograph of his friend R. K. Narayan for the cover of the book. I would have been literally lost in Mysore without the help and advice of Sridhara Murthy and his wife Sulochana. My wife Eleanor and I benefited from their warm hospitality, an immensely valuable tour of Narayan sites in Mysore, as well as guidance and assistance in any number of ways. Other friends and colleagues who gave crucial support and help include K. C. Belliappa, Shirley Chew, Sridevi and Seshadri Casuba, Gerald Dawe, Malcolm Sen and Smitha Seshadri. I am enormously grateful to Wendy Doniger who took the time in her immensely busy working life to read through my manuscript: the book is better for her comments and corrections. The incorrigible errors are all my own.

The book is dedicated to my sister Ruth who shares my love for Indian fiction in English.

Quotations from the works of R. K. Narayan appear by permission of Wallace Literary Agency, Inc. for the Estate of R. K. Narayan as follows: *The Bachelor of Arts* copyright 1937 by

R. K. Narayan; *My Dateless Diary* copyright © 1964 by R. K. Narayan; *The Dark Room* copyright 1938 by R. K. Narayan; *The English Teacher* copyright 1945 by R. K. Narayan; *The Financial Expert* copyright 1952 by R. K. Narayan; *Gods, Demons and Others* copyright © 1964 by R. K. Narayan; *The Grandmother's Tale: Three Novellas* copyright © 1993 by R. K. Narayan; *The Guide* copyright © 1958 by R. K. Narayan; *A Horse and Two Goats* copyright © 1970 by R. K. Narayan; *Indian Thought: a Miscellany* copyright © 1997 by R. K. Narayan; *The Mahabharata* copyright © 1978 by R. K. Narayan; *Malgudi Days* copyright © 1982 by R. K. Narayan; *The Man-Eater of Malgudi* copyright © 1961 by R. K. Narayan; *My Days: a Memoir* copyright © 1973, 1974 by R. K. Narayan; *The Painter of Signs* copyright © 1976 by R. K. Narayan; *The Ramayana* copyright © 1972 by R. K. Narayan; *Mr Sampath – the Printer of Malgudi* copyright 1949 by R. K. Narayan; *Swami and Friends* copyright 1935 by R. K. Narayan; *Talkative Man* copyright © 1986 by R. K. Narayan; *A Tiger for Malgudi* copyright © 1982 by R. K. Narayan; *Under the Banyan Tree* copyright © 1986 by R. K. Narayan; *The Vendor of Sweets* copyright © 1966 by R. K. Narayan; *Waiting for the Mahatma* copyright 1955 by R. K. Narayan; *The World of Nagaraj* copyright © 1990 by R. K. Narayan; *The Writerly Life* copyright © 2001 Estate of R. K. Narayan; *A Writer's Nightmare* copyright © 1988 by R. K. Narayan.

Biographical Outline

1906   10 October, born Rasipuram Krishnaswami Iyer Narayanaswami in Madras, third of eight children. Raised in Madras by his grandmother.

1921   Moves to Mysore where his father was Headmaster of Maharaja's Collegiate High School, attended by Narayan. Fails his first two attempts at entrance examination for college.

1924   First efforts at writing.

1926–30 Student at Maharaja's College, part of the University of Mysore.

1930   Graduates, after failing his BA at first attempt. After very brief unsuccessful spells as a schoolteacher, determines to become full-time writer. First newspaper articles published and short stories written.

1931–2 *Swami and Friends* written.

1934   Marries Rajam in Coimbatore. News reporter for *The Justice*. Collection of short stories shown to Graham Greene by Narayan's Oxford-based friend 'Kittu' Purna.

1935   At instigation of Greene, *Swami and Friends* published by Hamish Hamilton, under the name R. K. Narayan.

1936   Daughter Hema born.

1937   *The Bachelor of Arts* published by Nelson.

1938   *The Dark Room* published by Macmillan. Begins to write for *The Hindu*, the newspaper for which he will regularly write short stories and columns.

1939   His wife Rajam dies of typhoid. State-commissioned guidebook *Mysore* published.

1939–40 At seances in Madras, Narayan receives detailed communications from his dead wife, providing him with the basis for his autobiographical novel *The English Teacher*.

1940 While continuing to live with his daughter in the joint family home in Mysore, begins to travel often to Madras to broadcast radio talks.

1941 Turns down invitation to join the story department of Gemini Studios in Madras but will contribute to screenwriting for its producer Vasan for several years. Edits and publishes three issues of the quarterly *Indian Thought*.

1943 Publishes his first collection of short stories *Malgudi Days* under his own Indian Thought imprint in Mysore to be followed by *Dodu and Other Stories* and eventually Indian editions of all his novels.

1945 *The English Teacher* published by Eyre and Spottiswoode.

1947 *The Astrologer's Day and Other Stories* published by Eyre and Spottiswoode.

1948 Starts to build his own house in Yadavagiri, on the outskirts of Mysore.

1949 *Mr Sampath – Printer of Malgudi* published, drawing on his experiences as editor and screenwriter.

1952 *The Financial Expert* published.

1955 *Waiting for the Mahatma* published.

1956 Marriage of daughter Hema. First trip outside India on a Rockefeller Foundation Fellowship to visit the United States. Meets Graham Greene, long-term friend, supporter and editor, for the first time in London. Writes *The Guide* mostly in Berkeley, California.

1958 *The Guide* published.

1960 *The Guide* wins the Sahitya Akademi Award, annual prize awarded by the the Indian National Academy of Letters.

1961 *The Man-Eater of Malgudi* published by Heinemann, to become Narayan's major British publisher for the rest of his career.

1964 *My Dateless Diary*, an account of the 1956 American journey published. *Gods, Demons and Others*, his first

	collection of re-told Indian legends, published. Padma Bhushan Award for distinguished service to the nation.
1965	Hindi film of *The Guide* starring Dev Anand released; although Narayan dislikes it for the liberties taken with his novel, the film is highly successful.
1967	*The Vendor of Sweets* published.
1969	Writer-in-residence at the University of Missouri, Kansas City.
1970	*A Horse and Two Goats and Other Stories* published.
1972	*The Ramayana*, adaptation of the Tamil epic, published.
1974	*My Days*, autobiographical memoir published.
1976	*The Painter of Signs* published.
1977	*The Emerald Route*, travel essays about the state of Karnataka, published.
1978	*The Mahabharata* published.
1980	Receives the A. C. Benson medal, a lifetime achievement award from the Royal Society of Literature in Britain.
1981	Elected honorary member of the American Academy of Arts and Letters.
1982	*Malgudi Days*, anthology of short stories, published.
1983	*A Tiger for Malgudi* published.
1985	*Under the Banyan Tree and Other Stories*, second major anthology, published. Nominated to the Rajya Sabha, India's upper house of parliament, where he serves a six-year term, though only speaking once.
1986	*Talkative Man* published.
1987	Receives the Soviet Land Nehru Award.
1988	*A Writer's Nightmare*, a selection of his prose essays, published.
1989	Teaches at the University of Texas at Austin.
1990	*The World of Nagaraj*, his last novel, published. After an illness, settles in Madras with daughter Hema and her husband, his home for the rest of his life.
1992	*Grandmother's Tale* published in Mysore, to appear in Britain in *Grandmother's Tale: Three Novellas* in 1993.
1994	Death of his daughter Hema.
1996	Appointed as a Fellow of the Sahitya Akademi.

2000   Padma Vibhushan Award, India's second highest civilian honour.

2001   Death in Chennai (Madras) on 13 May.

Abbreviations

NOTE ON TEXTS AND REFERENCES

For the convenience of readers, I have chosen the most widely available texts of Narayan's novels in both Indian and British editions. Although the texts are rarely different in substance, where the pagination is different I have given both page references for quotations, the Indian edition always first.

BA	*The Bachelor of Arts* (1937; Chennai: Indian Thought Publications, 1956, repr. 2008; London: Vintage, 2000)
Dateless	*My Dateless Diary* (1964; New Delhi: Penguin, 1988)
DR	*The Dark Room* (1938; Chennai: Indian Thought Publications, 1956, repr. 2008; London: Vintage, 2001)
ET	*The English Teacher* (1945; Chennai: Indian Thought Publications, 1955, repr. 2008; London: Vintage, 2001)
FE	*The Financial Expert* (1952; Chennai: Indian Thought Publications, 1958, repr. 2008; London: Vintage, 2001)
G	*The Guide* (1958; Chennai: Indian Thought Publications, 1958, repr. 2008; London: Penguin, 1988)
GDO	*Gods, Demons and Others* (1964; Delhi: Vision Books, 1987)
GT	*Grandmother's Tale* (1992; Chennai: Indian

	Thought Publications, 1992, repr. 2008); *The Grandmother's Tale: Three Novellas* (London: Heinemann, 1993)
Indian Thought	*Indian Thought: a Miscellany* (New Delhi: Penguin, 1997)
Mahabharata	*The Mahabharata* (1978; London: Penguin, 2001)
Malgudi	*Malgudi Days* (1982; London: Penguin, 1984)
MD	*My Days: a Memoir* (1974; Chennai: Indian Thought Publications, 2006, repr. 2008; London: Penguin, 1989)
MM	*The Man-Eater of Malgudi* (1961; Chennai: Indian Thought Publications, 1968, repr. 2008; London: Penguin, 1983)
Nagaraj	*The World of Nagaraj* (1990; Chennai: Indian Thought Publications, n.d., repr. 2006; London: Vintage, 2001)
Nightmare	*A Writer's Nightmare* (New Delhi: Penguin, 1988)
PS	*The Painter of Signs* (1976; Chennai: Indian Thought Publications, n.d., repr. 2007; London: Penguin, 1982)
Ram & Ram	Susan Ram and N. Ram, *R. K. Narayan: the Early Years 1906–1945* (New Delhi: Viking Penguin, 1996)
Ramayana	*The Ramayana* (1972; London: Penguin, 1977)
Sam	*Mr Sampath – the Printer of Malgudi* (1949; Chennai: Indian Thought Publications, 1956, repr. 2008; London: Vintage, 2000)
SF	*Swami and Friends* (1935; Chennai: Indian Thought Publications, 1944, repr. 2008; London: Vintage, 2000)
Thieme	John Thieme, *R. K. Narayan* (Manchester: Manchester University Press, 2007)
Tiger	*A Tiger for Malgudi* (1983; Chennai: Indian Thought Publications, 1986, repr. 2007; London: Penguin, 1984)
TM	*Talkative Man* (1986; Chennai: Indian Thought Publications, 1986, repr. 2007; London: Penguin, 1987)

UBT	*Under the Banyan Tree* (1985; Chennai: Indian Thought Publications, 1992, repr. 2008; London: Penguin, 1987)
VS	*The Vendor of Sweets* (1967; Chennai: Indian Thought Publications, 1967, repr. 2008; London: Penguin, 1983)
WM	*Waiting for the Mahatma* (1955; Chennai: Indian Thought Publications, 1967, repr. 2008; London: Vintage, 2000)
Writerly	*The Writerly Life*, ed. S. Krishnan (New Delhi: Penguin, 2001)

Introduction

'R. K. Narayan, a Madras Indian who writes in English, has
few equals among modern novelists'. This was the view of the
Times Literary Supplement writer who contributed a page-length
overview of Narayan's work in 1958 shortly after his book *The
Guide* had been published.[1] Much more acclaim was to follow
with awards and prizes within India (the Sahitya Akademi
award for *The Guide* in 1960, the Padma Bhushan Award in
1964 and the Padma Vibhushan Award in 2000) and abroad
(the A. C. Benson medal in Britain in 1980, honorary member-
ship of the American Academy of Arts and Letters in 1981). He
was frequently nominated for the Nobel Prize for literature, his
name canvassed often enough as a likely contender to provoke
an uneasily dismissive essay from him (*Nightmare* 202–5).
Famously helped and supported through much of his career by
Graham Greene, he was admired by a wide range of fellow
writers including E. M. Forster, Saul Bellow, John Updike and
even (with important reservations) V. S. Naipaul. And past the
centenary of his birth in 2006, he continues to be read and his
influence acknowledged by a younger generation of Indian
writers into the twenty-first century.

Praise and appreciation for Narayan have not been lacking.
Yet it has been difficult to find the right terms to define his
distinction. The outstanding features of his work, gentle ironic
humour, simplicity and directness of style, low-key plot and
action, hardly sound like the characteristics of a major writer.
Early admirers and critics of Narayan tended to reach for
canonical Western comparisons to give a sense of his quality.
So Graham Greene was the first to suggest a likeness to
Chekhov that was much repeated in subsequent analyses: the

1

tragicomic poise of Narayan's tone, his detached lack of moralizing, his economical and suggestive style all could be seen as Chekhovian. The pioneering Indian critic K. R. S. Iyengar was only one of many to invoke Jane Austen: 'Narayan's is the art of resolved limitation and conscientious exploration; he is content, like Jane Austen, with a "little bit of ivory", just so many inches wide'.[2] Narayan's concentration on the single imagined town of Malgudi led to comparisons with Thomas Hardy's Wessex or, still more improbably, William Faulkner's Yoknapatawpha County.[3] The richness of his characterization was commonly referred to as Dickensian. These sorts of critical efforts to place Narayan within a landscape of writers more familiar to Western readers were matched by formalist studies of his skills and techniques. His pervasive irony in particular attracted attention and one whole book was devoted to his 'ironic vision'.[4]

Early critics and interpreters of Narayan tended to stress the universality of his work, whether by his resemblances to earlier British, European or American writers, or by his readily recognizable gifts as a writer of fiction in English. But from the beginning the distinctiveness of his Indian background was acknowledged as the necessary condition for the understanding of his work. In any history of the subject, Narayan is always bracketed with Mulk Raj Anand and Raja Rao as one of the three writers who essentially created the Indian novel in English in the 1930s. A key part of the success of his fiction was 'the authenticity and attractiveness of its Indian setting'.[5] Increasingly, however, it has been argued that without an understanding of Narayan's specific South Indian milieu, and the Hindu belief systems underpinning his writing, Western readers and critics will be disposed to misread his novels. So previous comparisons are shown to be unhelpful; in spite of superficial resemblances, Narayan is not really Chekhovian.[6] The inaction and passivity of the typical Narayan protagonist are to be seen as exemplary of Hindu fatalism. As V.S. Naipaul put it in an extremely influential critique, 'Narayan's novels are less the purely social comedies I had once taken them to be than religious books, at times religious fables, and intensely Hindu'.[7] Many Narayan critics have sought to elucidate these fables by uncovering the myths and legends lying below the secular surface stories. Narayan, earlier praised for his easy accessibility and the broad appeal of his humanist vision, has come to be viewed as a writer very much of his time and place. So the most recent major study of his work by John Thieme, while bringing to bear on Malgudi Michel Foucault's concept of *heterotopia*, analyses the novels in terms of their Tamil Brahmin contexts and intertexts (Thieme 11–15).

The puzzle of Narayan is that there is really no other writer quite like him and, though his South Indian background and Hindu culture are indeed crucial to the shaping of his work, the relation of that work to its contexts is never straightforward. As a result, in the book that follows I will be recurrently using contrasts as much as comparisons: how Narayan's representation of India is different from that of his Indian contemporaries but equally how unlike his fiction is to that of Western novelists. The distinction of Narayan is best understood in its distinctiveness. It is distinctive, also, in the relative homogeneousness of his work. Over the nearly sixty years of his writing life, he did undoubtedly change and develop, but change and development are not the most interesting features of his fiction: there are no striking shifts of style and theme. He early discovered his own imaginative territory and went on exploring and exploiting it for the rest of his career. Instead of a chronological organization of the book, therefore, I have built it around certain key issues and themes that are central for the appreciation of Narayan.

The first chapter is concerned with the creation of Malgudi and its distinguishing features exemplified in *Swami and Friends* (1935), *The Bachelor of Arts* (1937) and *The English Teacher* (1945). The second chapter tackles the much-debated issue of Narayan's apparent lack of political concern by considering politics and marriage in an early, middle and later novel: *The Dark Room* (1938), *Waiting for the Mahatma* (1955) and *The Painter of Signs* (1976). Hindu myth and legend are most prominent in three novels often considered Narayan's best: *The Financial Expert* (1952), *The Guide* (1958) and *The Man-Eater of Malgudi* (1961). The third chapter analyses how we should interpret these books' Hindu fables embedded as they are in a largely secular society realistically represented. Narayan has often been considered a conservative writer, his Malgudi an unchanging enclave protected against the disruptive forces of a wider modern world. In the fourth chapter this view is tested against two novels written almost twenty years apart, *Mr Sampath, Printer of Malgudi* (1949) and *The Vendor of Sweets* (1967). Narayan thought of himself as a storyteller and wrote several volumes of short stories as well as his fourteen novels. The final chapter of this book will be concerned with his styles of storytelling particularly in the experimental *A Tiger for Malgudi* (1983), *Talkative Man* (1986) and his last novella 'The Grandmother's Tale' (1992).

If this study differs from other introductions to Narayan's work in that it is not chronologically organized, it is also unusual in its lack of concern with critical evaluation, the assessment of the relative strengths and weaknesses of one novel or another. For the most part, I am happy to leave that to the judgement of Narayan's readers themselves who will no doubt have their own preferences. My concern rather is to look at the whole body of his fiction and to try to define what constitutes its distinguishing and distinctive features. As a long-term admirer of his writing, I believe this is the best way to encourage readers to read or re-read him, and that is the main objective of my book.

1

The Imagination of Malgudi

MAPPING

What is Malgudi and where is Malgudi? From *Swami and
Friends*, his first published book, to *The World of Nagaraj*
fifty-five years later, Malgudi remains so consistently the
location for Narayan's fiction that it begins to feel like a
recognizable place with a real-life counterpart. Anyone who
has read one Narayan novel will know to look out for the
landmarks of Malgudi: the railway station, so central to *The
Guide*, the Albert Mission College, where Chandran is a
student in *The Bachelor of Arts*, Krishnan a lecturer in *The
English Teacher*, the river Sarayu beside which so many of the
characters stroll of an evening, Nalappa's Grove on the other
side of the river, and the Mempi Hills beyond. We feel we
could find our own way around the different areas of Malgudi,
from the commercial centre of Market Road, through the
residential districts of Kabir Lane and Ellaman Street, to the
elite suburb of the Lawley Extension. Occasionally we are
given a suggestion of the historical evolution of Malgudi; *The
Guide* opens with Raju's memories of childhood before the
coming of the railway that appears to represent the transformation of a backward village into a modern town; we hear in *The
English Teacher* of a further building development, a New
Extension beyond the Lawley Extension. But for the most part
Malgudi appears solidly the same, its very unchanging stabil-
ity one of the attractions of Narayan's fiction, a topographical
comfort zone like Trollope's Barsetshire.

Yet Narayan always insisted that the place was purely
fictional and could not be placed in terms of the actual

geography of South India. He explained the origin of the name in an interview at the age of 90: as he worried about what to call his imagined place, 'the idea came to me – Malgudi just seemed to hurl into view. It has no meaning. There is a place called Lalgudi near Trichy and a place called Mangudi near Kumbakonam or somewhere. But Malgudi is nowhere'.[1] Both Trichy (now Tiruchirapalli) and Kumbakonam are in the modern state of Tamil Nadu, in the colonial period within the Presidency of Madras, and in fact Trichy is often a reference point as a major city within reach of Malgudi. Yet some of the main landmarks of Malgudi are readily identifiable with places in Mysore, the city where Narayan went to school and college and was to live for most of his life. The Albert Mission College, for instance, is based on the Maharaja's College of the University of Mysore where Narayan took his B.A. Mysore, now in the state of Karnataka, to the west of Tamil Nadu, was still a nominally independent state under the Wodeyar rajas until fully assimilated into the Republic of India in 1956. The language of Mysore is Kannada, while that of Madras (where Narayan lived as a child) and Tamil Nadu is Tamil.

Narayan's authoritative biographers Susan and N. Ram deny that Malgudi is essentially Mysore. It has neither the size, nor 'the princely trappings of Karnatak's second city'.

> It is also a place whose inhabitants are clearly, although not obtrusively, Tamil. This said, it is evident that Mysore has made significant inputs into what is the quintessential South Indian district town. Elements from Narayan's Madras childhood can also be detected along with impressions of Coimbatore and other urban settings . . . which he visited as a young man.[2]

Malgudi is a fictional composite of different places, Madras, Mysore and Coimbatore, also in Tamil Nadu, where he spent time with his sister. But even the formulation 'the quintessential South Indian district town' is questionable. For the size and scale and status of Malgudi are as hard to pin down as its position on the map. It often feels like a very small town indeed, hardly more than a village. The sketch-map drawn by Narayan's artist brother, the well-known Indian cartoonist, R. K. Laxman, as a frontispiece to *Waiting for the Mahatma* makes it look positively diminuitive.[3] It does not correspond to the topography implied in the novels either, putting the Lawley Extension close to the river rather than on the other side of town.[4] But then the sketch may only have been a tongue-in-cheek gesture to the literalism of readers who wanted Malgudi mapped out for them. All the same, it is disconcerting to come across references to Malgudi characters having to walk distances of miles between one place and another. The village-like scale of the town is suddenly stretched out towards the dimensions of a city. Some of the features drawn from Mysore equally belie the impression of an insignificant district town. The Albert Mission College, with its 200 graduates a year, the Lawley Extension as an enclave for upper civil servants, both imply a substantial urban community with a developed middle class. The iconic Malgudi railway station is based on the local Chamarajapuram station on a branch line in Mysore, not its main terminus, and in many ways Malgudi reflects a specific neighbourhood within the city rather than being a town on its own. We can see why Narayan himself was so resistant to attempts at a definitive cartography of Malgudi: 'To see an imaginary place so solidly presented with its streets and rivers and temples' was 'a petrification or fossilization of light wish-like things floating across one's vision while one is writing' (*Nightmare* 201).

Malgudi is, in fact, an imagined community in a sense very different from, almost antithetical to that popularized by Benedict Anderson. Anderson argued for the emergence of the modern concept of the nation at a point in the late eighteenth century when the development of mass print media made it possible for millions of people unknown to one another to imagine themselves as a community with shared beliefs and aspirations.[5] Narayan in Malgudi imagines a community sufficiently small and sufficiently local so that everyone knows one another, more or less. It is governed by its own specificities, which are not that of the nation as a whole. Narayan's characters rarely travel far outside their own environment, virtually never out of a restricted area of South India. Sriram's visit to Delhi towards the end of *Waiting for the Mahatma* is an exception that proves the rule; he feels totally alienated and estranged in the north. Yet the sense of the limited knownness of the Malgudi community is based on its social limitations. As Joyce creates a Dublin where it appears that everyone is familiar with one another by concentrating on a particular cross-section of the Catholic middle class, so Narayan's Malgudians are (for the most part) upper caste Hindus. Within Malgudi peons and servants appear only incidentally; there are occasional Muslims and Christians, and there must be untouchables to empty the latrines, but we rarely hear of them. And beyond Malgudi, there is the expanse of forest and jungle, the backward villages that expose to the central characters, whenever they venture out into them, just how limited and fragile their imagined community actually is.

DISCOVERY

In his autobiography, *My Days*, Narayan describes how he first conceived of Malgudi.

> On a certain day in September, selected by my grandmother for its auspiciousness, I bought an exercise book and wrote the first line of a novel; as I sat in a room nibbling my pen and wondering what to write, Malgudi with its little railway station swam into view, all ready-made, with a character called Swaminathan running down the platform peering into the faces of the passengers, and grimacing at a bearded face; this seemed to take me on the right track of writing, as day by day pages grew out of it linked to each other. (*MD* 87, 76–7)

It is a wonderful story of creative breakthrough, and the context is significant. Narayan had spent his early childhood with his grandmother in Madras; she had taken charge of him to afford relief to his mother of one member of her ever growing family in the remote village of Chennapatna in the state of Mysore where his father was headmaster. It was his grandmother who taught him his letters in Tamil, who made him learn 'Sanskrit *slokas* praising Sariswathi, the Goddess of Learning', and identify classical *ragas* (*MD* 9, 9). Her choice of the auspicious day on which to start his career as a novelist was itself auspicious. It is as though Malgudi arose directly out of the Tamil Hindu traditions of culture and belief he identified with his grandmother.

The process of arriving at that magical moment of inspiration, however, was a complicated and uncertain one. 'Writing in the beginning', he later confessed to his younger friend the photographer T. S. Satyan, 'was all frustration and struggle'.[6] His large family of five brothers and two sisters were Tamil speaking but, with a highly literate schoolteacher father who taught through English, they were early familiar with English as well. And after their father was transferred to Mysore to be headmaster of the Maharaja's Collegiate School (original of the Albert Mission School in *Swami and Friends*), the younger siblings grew up speaking Kannada as well. R. K. Laxman, the last of the children, remembers an easy atmosphere of trilingualism among his older brothers at home.[7] This did not stop Narayan from failing his university entrance examination in English. He was not an academically gifted student, always resistant to the systematic pedantry of the Indian education at the time. He managed to re-take his English examination and continue on to college and eventually to scrape his way through a BA though taking an extra year to do so, but his career options seemed limited. He was not going to become a successful administrator like his brother Srinivas who went into service in the palace secretariat of the Maharaja of Mysore. In *My Days* he gives a hilarious account of his two abortive attempts to become a schoolteacher like his father, in his father's old school at Chennapatna: he lasted just one day each time (*MD* 87–98, 77–86). Like so many would-be writers, he was a middle-class misfit, ill-adapted to any conventional profession, trying to find a vocation and a voice.

And yet, for all his initial failure to matriculate in English, it was English literature and literary culture that he devoured in the year's freedom given to him by that very failure, when he was out of school preparing to re-sit the examination. He spent hours walking around the beautiful Kukanahalli Tank, the large man-made reservoir near his home in Mysore, reading 'Keats, Shelley, Byron, and Browning' (*MD* 62, 56). He read through the novels of Scott and then 'picked up a whole row of Dickens and loved his London and the queer personalities therein. Rider Haggard, Marie Corelli, Molière, and Pope and Marlowe, Tolstoi, Thomas Hardy – an indiscriminate jumble; I read everything with the utmost enjoyment' (*MD* 65, 58–9).

His father kept the school library astonishingly well-stocked with current English and American periodicals: *The Strand Magazine, The Bookman, Harper's, Atlantic, American Mercury, Times Literary Supplement* and the *Manchester Guardian.* 'The London *Mercury,* with its orange cover and uncut pages, was especially welcome. I viewed J. C. Squire as if he were my neighbour' (*MD* 68, 61). He was the more indignant and hurt when his own first pieces, rhapsodic essays on 'Friendship' and 'Divine Music', were turned down by this 'neighbour' far away in London.

Narayan's predicament in 1930s Mysore was that of many writers beginning within a colonial/postcolonial context. His models and his medium all came from the literary centres of metropolitan London, an inheritance of canonized literature remote from his own life and experience. An early attempt to find a subject from within his own culture was no more successful, 'a play called *Prince Yazid,* the story of an independent-minded Mughal prince who was tortured and tormented by his father' (*MD* 85, 75). It was to languish unpublished for many decades in the files of his literary agent; to judge by his few published radio playlets, Narayan was never going to be a dramatist.[8] Narayan's struggle was to find his way from the condition of the 'provincial' to that of the 'parochial' writer, to use the terms of the Irish poet Patrick Kavanagh. Kavanagh, himself to provide an important role model for Seamus Heaney, defined the provincial as the writer who remained committed to the values of the literary metropolis to which he himself was peripheral, rather than trusting to the subject of his own local parish.[9] It was this transition, this access of confidence in his own local setting that was achieved when Narayan conceived of Malgudi.

And yet, of course, he was dependent on being published in Britain to achieve the recognition of an international readership. *Swami and Friends,* when completed, was sent to publisher after publisher in London and rejected by all of them. Narayan had reached the point of despair of instructing his Mysore friend Kittu Purnu (who was studying at Oxford) to dump it in the river after its last rejection, when Purnu gave it to Graham Greene instead, whose recommendation ensured its publication with Hamish Hamilton. Greene's sponsorship of

Narayan, whose manuscripts he continued to edit right through to the 1960s, was crucial to giving the Indian novelist standing in the English-speaking literary marketplace.[10] In a private letter he praised *Swami and Friends* as 'a book in ten thousand'[11] (a quotation inevitably used on almost every subsequent reprint), and in his fullest endorsement, spoke of his gratitude to Narayan, 'for he has offered me a second home. Without him I could never have known what it is like to be Indian' (Introduction to *BA* v).

This sort of patronage by the established British writer for the Indian novelist may sound slightly patronizing, even Orientalist, but it represents a real recognition of what Narayan achieved with the creation of Malgudi, even in his very first book. For *Swami and Friends* does indeed realize its environment and enable readers to live within it with a remarkable lack of self-consciousness. A contrast with two of the other landmark works of Indian fiction in English published at nearly the same time may bring this out. Mulk Raj Anand's *Untouchable* also appeared in London in 1935; once again, as with Narayan's work, it needed the support of a well-known English writer, in this case an introduction by E. M. Forster, to see print, after having been turned down by nineteen publishers.[12] The novel is a fierce political indictment of the position of India's underclass, the so-called 'untouchables' who are at the bottom of the caste system. As a day in the life of one such sweeper, it aims to make us feel with him the scorn, oppression and brutality with which he is treated. It was an important book in its time, inspired by Gandhi with the benefit of the Mahatma's own editorial advice, but its political good intentions fairly obviously interpose between reader and character. Raja Rao's *Kanthapura*, which followed in 1938, is a very different sort of experiment. Written as though in the voice of an old illiterate grandmother in the fictitious South Indian village that gives the novel its title, it makes use of an invented English based on the syntax of Kannada. This hybridized language, as Rao's Preface makes clear, represents an attempt to create a distinctive Indian English on the model of Irish or American non-standard English put to literary purposes. From its first sentence, the strangeness of the style, the emphasized remoteness of the setting, give it an outward-directed exoticism: 'Our village – I don't think you have ever heard of it – Kanthapura is its name, and it is in the province of Kara'.[13]

By contrast, the opening of *Swami and Friends* takes us inside the mentality of the young Malgudi schoolboy in a language that seems almost transparent in its simplicity:

> It was Monday morning. Swaminathan was reluctant to open his eyes. He considered Monday specially unpleasant in the calendar. After the delicious freedom of Saturday and Sunday, it was difficult to get into the Monday mood of work and discipline. He shuddered at the very thought of school: that dismal yellow building; the fire-eyed Vendanayagam, his class-teacher; and the headmaster with his thin long cane . . . (*SF* 1)

The names apart, this might be any reluctant schoolchild waking up to the dismal realities of Monday anywhere in the world. The social setting takes shape for us through the eyes of Swami for whom it is the known and the normal. The school he attends is the Albert Mission School, the Prince Consort's name in the title bespeaking its origins in the period of Christian evangelism. Narayan here was drawing, in all probability, on his own experience of the two Christian schools he attended in Madras (*MD* 10–11, 10–11; 51–3, 47–8). Swami gets his ear wrung by the fanatical Scripture teacher Mr Ebenezar, for challenging his anti-Hindu propaganda: '"If [Jesus] was a god, why did he eat flesh and fish and drink wine?"', objects Swami. 'As a brahmin boy it was inconceivable to him that a god should be a non-vegetarian' (*SF* 4). A stern letter from Swami's father to the headmaster complaining of the incident – 'This is not the place for me to dwell upon the necessity for toleration in these matters' (*SF* 5) – with a threat of withdrawing his sons from the school, has immediate effect. We are placed within a time when an Albert Mission School, whatever its Christian origins, must be careful not to offend the sensibilities of its well-to-do middle-class Hindu parents: Swami's father is a lawyer.

At the same time, there is social cachet attached to being an Albert Mission schoolboy. When Swami gets in trouble for joining in nationalist protests and has to transfer to the Board High School, he loses status with his friends, acquiring in their view, 'the Board High School air – by which was meant a certain slowness and stupidity engendered by mental decay' (*SF* 108). The special snobberies of school – Swami is ostracized by his former group of friends when he becomes devoted to the socially superior newcomer Rajam, son of the Police Superintendent – reflect the hierarchical stratifications of the adult society. Swami and his friend Mani are intensely nervous the first time they go to visit Rajam whose family lives in Lawley Extension. Sure enough, they are stopped by a police-man approaching his house, who then turns 'astonishingly aimiable' (*SF* 25) when he learns they are friends of Rajam. Rajam himself lords it over the household, sending orders to the cook to bring coffee and tiffin, and shouting rudely at him when he duly arrives. The cook is well able to deal with the young master's airs and graces, but we are made aware of an intensely status-conscious society in which bullying and syco-phancy are the norm.

Swami and Friends is a schoolboy book, hardly a novel, more a set of sketches without a continuous shaping narrative. Its original title was *Swami the Tate*, Swami's nickname as fast bowler for the MCC (Malgudi Cricket Club) based on the then famous English cricketer Maurice Tate. The change in title, made at the suggestion of Graham Greene and the publisher, Hamish Hamilton, was intended to align the book with a western tradition of schoolboy fiction going back to *Stalky & Co* (Thieme 25). In fact, it brings out by contrast just how different Narayan's work is from the ethos of Kipling or indeed other English school stories with which it has been compared. Although Stalky, M'Turk and Kipling's autobiographical stand-in Beetle, may seem dissidents and rebels in the fictional version of the real-life United Services College, the book's epilogue shows just how well Stalky's heroic individualism was fitting him for the service of the Empire. It is never clear for what (if anything) Swami is being fitted by his schooling.

The book is in some ways closer to the William stories of Richmal Crompton, with which it has also been compared.[14] Like William, Swami the schoolboy is ironically observed from an implied adult standpoint, as he continually runs foul of the world of education and grown-ups which he so signally fails to understand. There is one set-piece, in which Swami's would-be cricket team write to a Madras sports shop for equipment, observed with a Crompton-like facetiousness at the boys' ignorance of the correct formal language:

> Dear Sir,
>   Please send to our team two junior willard bats, six balls, wickets and other things quick. It is very urgent. We shall send you money afterwards. Don't fear. Please be urgent.
>   Yours obediently,
>   CAPTAIN RAJAM (Captain)   (*SF* 117)

But even there the irony cuts more than one way. When the boys receive a proper formal letter back to the captain replying that Messrs. Binns 'would be much obliged to him if he would kindly remit 25 per cent with the order and the balance could be paid against the V.P.P. of the railway receipt' (*SF* 119), they are thoroughly baffled. Even after they turn up the meaning of 'obliged' in the dictionary, Mani, the 'Mighty Good-For-Nothing' of the group, 'was none the wiser. He felt that it was a meaningless word in that place' (*SF* 119). And of course he is right. The comic perspective allows us to see the fossilized inertness of this sort of commercial jargon as much as the boys' naïve lack of sophistication.

The pleasure of *Swami and Friends* derives from the distance the narrator maintains from the child's-eye view of the young Swami. But that distance is never stably fixed with the knowing assurance of the adult. Narayan makes use of the freedom of the free indirect style, which was to become his hallmark, the third-person narrative that is both inside and outside the consciousness of his protagonist. So, for instance, a process of miniaturization allows us to participate in Swami's emotions as he sets a paper boat with an ant on it to sail down the gutter running past his house:

> He watched in rapture its quick motion. He held his breath when the boat with its cargo neared a danger zone formed by stuck up bits of straw and other odds and ends. The boat made a beautiful swerve to the right and avoided destruction. It went on and on.   (*SF* 31–2)

The reader shares Swami's rapture, the anxiety and the sense of loss when at last 'the boat and its cargo were wrecked beyond recovery. He took a pinch of earth, uttered a prayer for the soul of the ant, and dropped it into the gutter' (*SF* 32). A delicate irony plays about the Hindu belief that any living thing may have a soul on its cycle of reincarnation, lightly implied in the improvised funeral ceremony for the ant.

Malgudi is a Hindu world shaped by Brahmin Hindu practice and belief, but from the beginning it is observed as a secular social comedy. In *The Bachelor of Arts*, for instance, the family of Chandran, undergraduate successor to Swami, is outraged by the continued depredations of a thief who comes each night and steals the flowers from their carefully cultivated garden. The mother is left with no flowers for her *puja*, the daily act of worship in the home. Father and son set themselves to stay up and catch the culprit. However, the scene changes when they discover who he is: 'The light showed the thief to be a middle-aged man, bare bodied, with matted hair, wearing only a loin-cloth. The loin-cloth was ochre-coloured, indicating that he was a *sanyasi*, an ascetic' (*BA* 43, 75). The mother is immediately disposed to back off – 'She was seized with fear now. The curse of a holy man might fall on the family' – but the brash young Chandran takes a modern and cynical line: 'What, Mother, you are frightened of every long hair and ochre dress you see'. He cross-questions the thief, 'If you are really a holy man, why should you do this?' But the *sanyasi* replies unanswerably:

> 'What have I done?' asked the thief.
> 'Jumping in and stealing the flowers'.
> 'If you lock the gate, how else can I get in than by jumping over the wall? As for stealing flowers, flowers are there, God-given. What matters it whether you throw the flowers on the gods, or I do it. It is all the same'. (*BA* 43, 76)

The clash between this devout logic and the proprietorial attitude of the family is resolved when the *sanyasi* agrees for the future to take only a few of the flowers, leaving enough for the mother's *puja*.

As in many other cultures, the women of Malgudi tend to be the more devout, the men more disposed towards modern rationalism. The grandmothers, in particular, based on the archetype of Narayan's own grandmother in Madras, are the

15

standard representatives of traditional Hindu attitudes, the repositories of inherited myth and folklore, and corresponding-ly the most remote from Anglicized colonial culture. So, for instance, Swami is shocked at his Granny's ignorance of cricket: she has never heard of the great bowler Maurice Tate, after whom he is so gloriously nicknamed. In the political context of *Waiting for the Mahatma*, this opposition of the rebellious Sriram and his conservative grandmother is put to allegorical use. But Narayan, devout Hindu though he was himself, always places religious practice and belief within a social and material world. A representative moment comes early in *The Bachelor of Arts*, when Chandran comes home late, eager to go out to the cinema, impatient to get through his dinner:

> He then gave a shout, 'Mother!' which reached her as she sat in the back veranda, turning the prayer beads in her hands, looking at the coconut trees at the far end of the compound. As she turned the beads, her lips uttered the name of Sri Rama, part of her mind busied itself with thoughts of her husband, home, children, and relatives, and her eyes took in the delicate beauty of coconut trees waving against a starlit sky. (*BA* 12, 29–30)

This is not intended in any way to expose the mother's prayer as merely mechanical, but rather to show the nature of experience as 'incorrigibly plural', to use MacNeice's famous phrase.[15]

Swami and Friends, slight schoolboy book as it may appear, yet established the territory of Malgudi and the narrative configuration that were to provide the basis for most of Narayan's fiction. A normative social setting is sketched in, with Swami, home, family, the experience of school, his little gang of friends in which he holds an assured position. There follows disruption, often provoked by the arrival of an outsider, in this case Rajam, the admired new boy, who upsets the dynamics of the status quo. The disturbance rises to a crisis in which the protagonist is forced to leave Malgudi and the assurance of his ordinary self altogether. Swami, who has been virtually expelled from the Albert Mission School, gets into serious trouble at the Board High School also, and feels he has no alternative but to leave home. Although he only goes missing for a day and a night, Swami's sense of alienation and despair is well realized, and this flight from the security of the normal becomes a standard trajectory in the later novels. Equally standard, however, is the return to normality at the end, the pattern which is most simply summed up as order/disorder/order.

It is a pattern which has been taken to reflect Narayan's inherent social conservatism, with Malgudi the assured norm to which his protagonists, like Narayan's own readers in successive novels, inevitably come back. Even *Swami and Friends*, however, feels less comfortable than that would suggest. It is partly a matter of narrative discontinuities, the lack of expected story shapes. Inevitably, Swami runs away from home on the night before the 'MCC' face their big cricket match; the team is entirely dependent on his bowling skills for success. The very chapter titles seem to build the suspense: 'Swami disappears'; 'The day of the match'; 'The return'. In a conventional school story, like P. G. Wodehouse's early public-school cricketing books (an obvious influence here), Swami would miraculously arrive back in time and the match would be won in the final over by his triumphant bowling. That is precisely what does not happen in Narayan. A woebegone Swami is returned to his frantically worried family just too late to take part in the match which is lost as a result. The book ends with Swami desperately trying to reconcile himself with his adored Rajam, who is leaving Malgudi for good, but who will have nothing to do with Swami since his desertion of the cricket team. That scene at the railway station, which was Narayan's first imagination of Malgudi, is the scene of Swami's hopeless hunt for Rajam in the crowd at the end of the book. They do not meet, there is no touching farewell; the deliberately inconclusive anti-climactic ending is again characteristic of Narayan. Though Malgudi is realized as a vividly peopled community, such a community does not protect the individual within it from irresolvable insecurities of the self.

GROWING UP

Swami and Friends, together with *The Bachelor of Arts* (1937) and Narayan's fourth novel, *The English Teacher* (1945) form what amounts to an autobiographical trilogy. The names and family background of the central characters in each book change. Swami's father is a stern lawyer, sharply authoritarian in the home; the impulsive student Chandran has much more indulgent parents, the father, a retired District Magistrate, inclined to humour his son; the parents of Krishnan, the English teacher, do not actually live in Malgudi but in a village some distance away, with only occasional visits possible from Krishnan's mother when she is not engaged nursing his semi-invalid father. But the books move on logically one from another and in each case draw on Narayan's own experience. Swami attends the Albert Mission School, of which the real-life equivalent was the Maharaja's Collegiate School, where Narayan's father was headmaster. Chandran studies at the Albert Mission College, the counterpart of the Maharaja College where Narayan took his degree. And in *The English Teacher*, Narayan's most explicitly autobiographical novel, based as it is on the tragic early death of his wife and its aftermath, Krishnan is a lecturer at the Albert Mission College, where the members of staff, the self-important Principal Professor Brown and the pedantic Assistant English Professor Gajapathi, are carried over from the earlier book. The three novels taken together could be read as an Indian equivalent to Tolstoy's memoir-cum-fiction *Childhood, Boyhood, Youth*, the writer's working through of his own experience of growing up.

Yet there are key differences from the classic English language examples of the *Bildungsroman*, the autobiographically based novel of development: *David Copperfield, A Portrait of the Artist as a Young Man* or *Sons and Lovers*. Narayan certainly drew upon his own background and his own early life throughout the books. But the central figures are not so clearly to be identified with the author as they are in most such fiction. So, for example, in creating *Swami and Friends*, it is likely that he drew upon the experiences of his brother Laxman, eighteen years younger than himself, who was still at school at the time the book was being written. Some of Narayan's earliest stories were certainly based on Laxman's life rather than his own.[16] Chandran is a mediocre student in *The Bachelor of Arts*, as Narayan himself was, but without the author's writing ambitions. These are laid off instead on the semi-comic subordinate character Mohan, poverty-stricken author of lugubrious pastiche poems. It is he who is made to speak for the discouraged Mysore author, doomed to write in spite of continuous rejections:

> 'By every post I receive my poems back', said the poet. 'For the last five years I have been trying to get my poems accepted. I have tried almost all the papers and magazines in the world – England, America, Canada, South Africa, Australia, and our own country.... I can no more help writing than I can help breathing.... I shall go on writing till my fingers are paralysed.... I hope some day I shall come across an editor or publisher who is not stupid.' (BA 86, 50)

Later in the novel, Mohan does find work: 'I am now the Malgudi correspondent of the *Daily Messenger* of Madras. They have given me the whole district. They pay me three-eight per column of twenty-one inches' (BA 106, 62). Again Narayan gives to Mohan his own first job as a journalist, local Mysore news reporter for the Madras-based paper *The Justice*, and exactly his own rate of pay for that work, three rupees eight annas a column (MD 125, 110).

Krishnan in *The English Teacher* is evidently close to Narayan's experience and does have (constantly frustrated) ambitions as a poet. But these novels are never portraits of the artist as a young man, never centrally concerned with the emergence of the distinctive writerly temperament. In Joyce's *Portrait* or Lawrence's *Sons and Lovers*, the focus is always on the formation of the individual as he grows towards the self-conscious awareness of himself and his environment that will allow the writer to write, or in the case of Lawrence's Paul Morel, the painter to paint. Narayan chooses much more generic figures for central characters, not set apart from their community by a divergent sensibility, but representative agents within it. More broadly, the ideas of selfhood and individuality shaping his fiction are different from the European idea of development, the *Bildung* implicit in the *Bildungsroman*. We watch David Copperfield or Jane Eyre grow from childhood through the traumatic experiences of adolescence, young manhood or womanhood, towards a stable maturity from which these experiences are retrospectively observed: stage by stage, they develop from ignorance to knowledge, from helpless suffering to the assured possession of the self. There is no real equivalent to that graded process of maturation in Narayan, nor the prospect of a settled ego as narrative endpoint. This is in part because of the underpinning in Narayan's fiction of the classical Hindu concept of a man's life divided into four stages. Lakshmi Holmström provides a useful outline of the successive series of *asrama*: 'Asrama ideally divides a man's life into studenthood or apprenticeship, the status of a householder and finally renunciation of the world, with a shadowy intermediary stage of withdrawal before the last'.[17] The first stages in this scheme, and particularly the rites of passage from the first to the second, can be traced in Swami's schooldays, Chandran's changed status from student through graduate to newly married man, Krishnan's establishment as full householder when he moves from living in the College hostel to setting up house with his wife. In such a view of man's development – and it is always male-centered – maturation is necessarily much less individual and much more a matter of predetermined functional progression. However, Narayan plays games with the system when he has the young Chandran, disappointed in love, renounce his worldly life, taking to the road as an exceedingly premature *sanyasi*.[18] In fact, the principle of progression in Narayan is always problematic and the several states of studenthood, householding and withdrawal from the world are never treated as the clearly marked off stages of growth that the four-part paradigm suggests.

Education itself, whether at school or college, is rendered with deeply ironic scepticism. An early comic vignette of the puzzled Swami, faced with an arithmetic problem by his father, is typical.

'Rama has ten mangoes with which he wants to earn fifteen annas. Krishna wants only four mangoes. How much will Krishna have to pay?'
Swaminathan gazed and gazed at this sum, and every time he read it, it seemed to acquire a new meaning. He had the feeling of having stepped into a fearful maze . . .
His mouth began to water at the thought of mangoes. He wondered what made Rama fix fifteen annas for ten mangoes. What kind of a man was Rama? (*SF* 86)

At a complete loss, he asks his father 'if the mangoes were ripe', but he is told to concentrate on the sum.

> Swaminathan felt utterly helpless. If only Father would tell him whether Rama was trying to sell ripe fruits or unripe ones! . . . He felt strongly that the answer to this question contained the key to the whole problem. It would be scandalous to expect fifteen annas for ten unripe mangoes. But even if he did, it wouldn't be unlike Rama, whom Swaminathan was steadily beginning to hate and invest with the darkest qualities. (*SF* 87)

Swami's childish inability to grasp the abstract mathmatical principles involved in the problem, his impulse to turn it into a real-life situation with all its variables, are representative of Narayan's distrust of the merely conceptual, his imaginative investment in circumstantial actuality.

Narayan's students are dreamers, recurrently resolving to work determinedly to fixed timetables, but always getting caught up in whatever distractions offer. The glimpses that we are given of the exam-driven educational system, with its heavily colonial syllabus so alien to the Indian students who must study it, makes such distractedness easy to understand. Chandran tries to decide how to divide up his available revision time between 'Modern History, Ancient History, Political Theories, Greek Drama, Eighteenth-century Prose, and Shakespeare' (*BA* 39, 18) all of them to be mugged up out of prescribed textbooks. Those textbooks are occasionally put to practical uses: Krishnan discovers that the only thing that will silence his erratic alarm clock in the morning is the fat volume of Taine's *History of English Literature*. It comes in just as handy when he needs something to prop up his shaving-mirror in the bathroom: 'Taine every time', he mutters to himself (*ET* 22, 18).[19] Krishnan, drafting his letter of resignation from his post as college teacher to the English Principal, produces a vehement denunciation of an education that 'had reduced us to a nation of morons; we were strangers to our own culture and camp followers of another culture, feeding on leavings and garbage' (*ET* 178, 173). The only function of such a system was to create 'efficient clerks for all your business and administrative offices' (*ET* 179, 174).

Such sentiments may carry much of the weight of the

author's own feeling; he once wrote an essay on 'My Educational Outlook' summing it up as 'anti-educational'. 'I am not averse to enlightenment, but I feel that the entire organization, system, outlook and aims of education are hopelessly wrong from beginning to end'.[20] Yet, in the novel, Krishnan tears up his drafted letter, reacting against his own rhetoric as 'the repetition of ideas uttered a hundred times before. It looked like the rehash of an article entitled "Problems of Higher Education", which appeared again and again in a week-end educational supplement' (ET 179, 174). Narayan's resistance to the educational system is not primarily anti-colonial but more broadly anti-intellectual. The phenomenal embeddedness of lived experience is the only truth; any other sort of knowledge runs the risk of turning into a learned off rigmarole. On this basis of understanding, the sort of mental growth and development characteristic of other autobiographical fiction is ruled out. We never see Chandran or Krishnan altered under the impact of books or ideas as Stephen Dedalus is by reading Byron or Pater or Aquinas. Instead, narrative discontinuities tend to jump us from one moment in the lives of the characters to a later one. Part One of *The Bachelor of Arts* immerses us in the experience of Chandran as a final-year undergraduate, speaking at the debating society, on a night out with his best friend at the cinema, the febrile anxieties and elations of student activity distracting him from studying for his exams. Part Two then begins 'Within six months of becoming a graduate Chandran began to receive suggestions from relatives and elderly friends of the family as to what he should do with himself' (BA 91, 52). He arrives at this new status as the 'bachelor of arts' of the title without any plotted sense of how he got there.

Part Two of the novel is in fact taken up with Chandran's attempt to move from student to householder – an aborted attempt as it turns out. The system of arranged marriages, as has often been pointed out, works to deprive the Indian novelist of one of the standard narrative concerns of most western fiction writers, the emotional developments attendant on the protagonist's first love affairs. The whole protracted process of meeting, varying interactions, growth of feeling over time, which animate any number of English novels from Jane

Austen on, can hardly happen when marriage is a matter of parental negotiation rather than personal choice.[21] Chandran actually tries to challenge that system, by himself initiating a marriage proposal with a girl he has seen by the riverbank and with whom, on the basis of no actual acquaintance, he has fallen besottedly in love. Narayan here drew upon his own experience with Rajam, the woman who was to become his wife. When staying with his married sister in Coimbatore, 'One day, I saw a girl drawing water from the street-tap and immediately fell in love with her. Of course, I could not talk to her. I learned later that she had not even noticed me passing and repassing in front of her while she waited to fill the brass vessels' (MD 117, 103). Against all normal custom, Narayan himself proposed marriage to the father and persisted in his resolution to marry Rajam in spite of an initial conflict in their horoscopes. It is just such an astrological incompatibility that prevents Chandran from marrying his adored Malathi; she is quickly married off to someone else within the brief prescribed period immediately following puberty – Malathi is just fifteen – after which a girl becomes increasingly unmarriageable. In his autobiography, Narayan never comments explicitly on the tragic irony of the fact that the consequence of the mismatched horoscopes projected for the fictional Chandran-Malathi marriage, 'It kills the wife soon after the marriage' (BA 145, 88), became the catastrophe of his own life when his beloved Rajam died of typhoid in 1939.[22]

Chandran is left utterly desolate as a result of the failure to marry Malathi who has become an obsession. The loss of his love precipitates a loss in his sense of his own identity. He is sent off to stay with an uncle in Madras to recover, but cannot face his relations, disappears at the railway station and in his anguish tries to imagine what to do. Narayan manages to convey the depth and reality of Chandran's despair, while preserving an ironic distance. Alone in a hotel for the first time in his life, he is adopted by the drunken Kailas, the first of many such characters in Narayan, all more or less modelled on the author's own uncle, a highly successful car salesman whose drinking made him the black sheep of the family (MD 101–6, 89–94). There is a wonderful funny exchange when the horrified Chandran refuses a drink on the grounds that he had 'made a vow never to touch alcohol in my life, before my mother'.

> This affected Kailas profoundly. He remained solemn for a moment and said: 'Then don't. Mother is a sacred object. It is a commodity whose value we don't realize as long as it is with us. One must lose it to know what a precious possession it is. If I had my mother I should have studied in a college and become a respectable person.' (BA 161–2, 98–9)

Even in this extremity, the graduate Chandran remains just such a 'respectable person', a nicely brought up Brahmin boy, appalled at being in the presence of someone who drinks alcohol and goes with prostitutes. A day and a night of this company is all the *Walpurgisnacht* Chandran can endure.

He literally does not know where to go or what to do, caught between waves of homesickness for Malgudi and the horror of imagining Malathi there, married to someone else. He gets on a train to a random destination, but as soon as he is on it, he decides it is a mistake, looking at the yellow ticket in his hand: 'He was not going to be tyrannized by that piece of yellow cardboard into taking a trip to Bezwada' (BA 169–70, 104). He jumps out of the carriage before the train leaves the station. It is at this point, on impulse, that he decides to have his head shaved, don the ochre robe, and go on the road as a *sanyasi*. It has a certain logic to it for someone of Chandran's background, though even the barber who shaves him protests that it is the wrong time: 'Master, at your age!' (BA 171, 105). The admired persona of the *sanyasi*, 'one who had renounced the world and was untouched by its joys and sorrows' (BA 174, 107), represents the appropriate form of self-punishment for Chandran in his distressed state. But Narayan makes it clear that his is not the spiritual motivation of the usual *sanyasi*:

> Chandran's renunciation was not of that kind. It was an alternative to suicide. Suicide he would have committed but for its social stigma. Perhaps he lacked the barest physical courage that was necessary for it. He was a *sanyasi* because it pleased him to mortify his flesh. His renunciation was a revenge on society, circumstances, and perhaps, too, on destiny. (BA 176, 108)

In this state of chosen self-abnegation Chandran wanders for eight months through a waste of places almost as lacking in identity as himself: 'One town was very much like another: the same bazaar street, hair-cutting saloons, coffee hotels, tailors squatting before sewing-machines, grocers, Government officials, cycles, cars and cattle' (BA 174, 107). Malgudi as the archetypal South Indian provincial town may have its charms as known territory, but the endless replication of such places in all their anonymity across the vast space of the country threatens any sense of individuality. It is in a tiny remote village that Chandran comes to himself, and does so for significant reasons. He is initially flattered by the seriousness with which he is treated by the villagers: 'Master, our village is so unlucky that few come this way. Bless us with your holy presence for some more days, we beg of you' (BA 178, 109–10). But then the villagers' very humble neediness makes him ashamed of the falseness of his disguise: 'Sitting in the dark, he subjected his soul to a remorseless vivisection. From the moment he had donned the ochre cloth to the present, he had been living on charity, charity given in mistake, given on the face value of a counterfeit. He had been humbugging through life' (BA 180, 111).

This episode very obviously anticipates the situation in Narayan's great novel *The Guide*. But Raju, the guide, is a professional impersonator, someone who constantly shifts his shape for his own ends, the involuntary role of guru only one of the many such roles he has played, and he exploits it as he has done his acts as tourist guide or dance impresario. With Chandran the guileless veneration of the villagers brings him back to a proper sense of his home values of honesty and self-respect, and he recoils against his own act of pretence. Yet the 'remorseless vivisection' to which Chandran subjects himself is not quite as searingly truthful as he would like to think. He quickly slides into seeking someone to blame for his degradation, for the suffering he will have caused his parents:

> The more he reflected on this, the greater became his anger with Malathi. It was a silly infatuation. Little sign did she show of caring for a fellow. . . . She had only been playing with him, the devil. Women were like that, they enjoyed torturing people. (BA 180–1, 111–12)

'Malathi' as love object had been a pure projection of Chandran's desiring imagination in the first place; now she becomes the demon responsible for all his troubles. There is virtually never in Narayan a firm ground of assured identity from which the self can safely judge the self.

Chandran returns home to a prodigal's welcome, easily regaining his old position in the family. Even before he set out on his career as anonymous *sanyasi* he had sent his parents a reassuring postcard urging them not to worry about him. In the book's final Part Four, he settles down to a satisfactory adult career. He manages to acquire a job as distribution agent for a Madras newspaper by an Indian process of networking, the influence of friends of family friends, which is observed with wryly deadpan satire. Somewhat surprisingly, he makes a great success of it, showing a degree of enterprise, energy and initiative one would not have expected from the moony Chandran of the opening section of the book. Although he professes a lifelong aversion to the very idea of love, it takes little persuasion from his friend Mohan, and in the end the toss of a coin, for him to go along with his parents' tentative suggestion of marriage. And soon he is as passionately in love with his bride-to-be, Susila, as he previously was with Malathi – indeed more so.

> The music of the word 'Susila' rang in his ears. Susila, Susila, Susila. Her name, music, figure, face, and everything about her was divine. Susila, Susila – Malathi, not a spot beside Susila; it was a tongue-twister; he wondered why people liked that name. (*BA* 258, 162)

The book ends with him married to Susila and so utterly devoted to her that a few days without a letter from her – she is still living with her parents – sends him into such a fever of anxiety that he sets out immediately to find out if she has not fallen ill.

The vagaries of the young man in love – that may seem to be the substance of *The Bachelor of Arts*. They are specifically the vagaries of such a young man in India where, with any personal communication between boy and girl disallowed, love must be vested in someone more or less unknown. This necessarily raises issues about possible distinctions between infatuation, mere calf love and the 'real thing'. Is Chandran's feeling for Susila his bride any truer and more sincere that his passion for the chimerical Malathi? Or put the other way, is his love for Malathi and his anguish at losing her, to be dismissed as wholly unreal? A comparison with a standard English *Bildungsroman* may once again show the difference of Narayan's fiction. David Copperfield marries twice, the first time to the pretty but empty-headed Dora who conveniently dies and leaves him free to marry the morally superior Agnes, with whom he has long been in love and with whom he will share the happy-ever-after of the companionate marriage. Presupposed in such a novel is a paradigm of development in which the young man's superficial fancy is replaced by the depth of a true love relationship. No such secure pattern of maturing can be traced through *The Bachelor of Arts*. Yes, Chandran does grow up, takes his place in an adult world of work and gets married, but how really changed is he by that process? His later married self seems as impulsive, as uncertain, as emotionally unstable as the dreamy student, or the love-struck young graduate. Such a condition of the ego seems chronic in Malgudi, not merely a stage on the road to a more stable state of 'maturity'. The issue of the potential development of the self, and the nature of love within that development, are fully tested within *The English Teacher*.

DEATH

The English Teacher has to be seen as anomalous and problematic in any view of Narayan's body of fiction. In many ways, it does look like the third in the autobiographical trilogy that began with *Swami and Friends*. The newly-married Chandran in his early twenties is replaced by Krishnan who is already a father and about to turn thirty. And Krishnan achieves the full status of householder denied to Chandran. Though the book opens with Krishnan, like Chandran, still living apart from his wife, they are soon reunited and enabled to set up house together. The wives in the two books even have the same name, Susila. In *The English Teacher*, we are shown the romantic raptures of the bridegroom changed into the domestic delight of the newly settled husband and father. In fact, one of the strengths of the book is its portrayal of married love from

27

within such a Malgudi household: Krishnan's pleasure in the rhythms of its life; Susila's fiercely determined management of the household budget; the mildly disruptive arrival of an 'old lady' – she is never given a name – a widowed dependant sent by Krishnan's mother to help out; the occasional squabbles of the loving couple in their period of adjustment. It gives social and psychological substance to the condition of 'householder' in the traditional four stage Indian division of life.

And yet the book is made wholly different from *Swami and Friends* or *The Bachelor of Arts* by its direct relationship to Narayan's own experience. That difference is signalled from the beginning by the adoption of the first person narrative: 'I was on the whole very pleased with my day – not many conflicts and worries, above all not too much self-criticism' (*ET* 5, 1). The gap between narrator and protagonist represented by the free indirect style used in the earlier books – and most of the later ones also – is narrowed. Ironic distance is also diminished as a result; we share Krishnan's deadened ennui in the classroom and it is from Krishnan's exacerbated point of view that we watch the ridiculous staff room argument about the importance of English orthography (*ET* 15–17, 11–12). But it is the turn in the narrative in the second half of the book that makes it so unlike any other novel Narayan ever wrote. As he declared in *My Days*: '*The English Teacher* is autobiographical in content, very little of it being fiction' (*MD* 150, 131). Susila dies of typhoid, as Rajam, Narayan's wife, had died five years before the book was written. Narayan even made use of his own diary in writing the novel. The aftermath of desolation, followed by the consolation discovered in communication with the dead wife through a spiritualistic medium, are all based on the writer's personal experience.

As a result, it has been hard to know what to make of the book. 'From its earliest reviewers onwards, many of *The English Teacher*'s readers have seen it as a broken-backed novel' (Thieme 54).[23] Narayan himself most suggestively describes the nature of this reaction:

> The book falls in two parts – one is domestic life and the other half is 'spiritual'. Many readers have gone through the first half with interest and the second half with bewilderment and even resent-

ment, perhaps feeling that they have been baited with the domestic picture into tragedy, death, and nebulous, impossible speculations. . . . most readers resist, naturally, as one always does, the transition from life to death and beyond. (*MD* 151, 132)

The spiritualist material, so embarrassing to most western readers, appears to be no more acceptable to Indian critics. Even as devoted an admirer as the pioneering scholar C.D. Narasimhaiah offers a mild reproof to the novelist for turning 'to the occult as a substitute for the profoundly spiritual which his own heritage could have offered in abundance'.[24]

Uneasiness with the spiritualist material apart, it is the treatment of death that is so disconcerting in the novel. 'Most readers', Narayan says, 'resist . . . the transition from life to death and beyond'. True, but that transition seems especially out of place in the context of the fictional space that is Malgudi. Deaths do occasionally occur in Narayan's novels, most notably in the last lines of *Waiting for the Mahatma* and (arguably) in the last lines of *The Guide*. In both cases, however, they take place away from Malgudi itself. For Malgudi is a comic enclave, protected as comedy normally is from the terminal realities of fatal illness and mortality. Within such a space a whole range of painful human experiences and emotions may be rendered: stress, anxiety, extremes of fear and anger, but not the blank desolation of facing the annihilation of life itself. It is this that Krishnan must work through in the second half of *The English Teacher* in some other mode than that normally used in Narayan's fiction. And the book is perhaps most usefully seen not merely as a therapeutic aid to the author to take him through the despair of grief (though it may well have been that) but in its death-struck tragic consciousness as an illumination in contrast to the normal comic constitution of Malgudi.

Right through the opening part of the book, the life of Malgudi is rendered in its usual detailed actuality. The hostel where Krishnan lives initially, with the daily queue for the bathroom in the morning, Krishnan's mad worries while he waits at the station for the arrival of Susila and the child, his 'monthly salary' of 'ten ten-rupee notes bulging in an envelope' (*ET* 37, 33) that he proudly hands over to his wife, all contribute to the earthed reality of ordinary life. On their daughter's third birthday, Krishnan's father offers to advance them the money to buy or build a house of their own. The couple make an excited excursion across town to the New Extension to view a house, for which Sastri, a logic teacher colleague of Krishnan, is acting as agent:

> He was the moving spirit of this new extension, secretary of the Building and Acquisition Society, and a most energetic 'extender'. No one could have believed he had so much business capacity – his main occupation being logic. He was a marvellous man – a strange combination of things, at one end 'undistributed middle', 'definition of knowledge', syllogisms', and at the other he had the spirit of a pioneer. (*ET* 56, 52)

Narayan allows no hint of tragic foreknowledge about this outing, which proves to be the last normal day Krishnan and Susila share; it is a festive holiday as they eat, very unusually, in a restaurant, walk by the river, plan their future together in their grand new house. We can see why readers may experience 'bewilderment and even resentment' when this tender domestic comedy turns without warning into the painful scenes of the wife's protracted illness and death.

In the successive stages of that illness, Narayan initially maintains a distanced narratorial estrangement, as we see the assured doctor in his dispensary – 'He might have been a great machine dispensing health, welfare and happiness' (*ET* 73, 68) – and his very different manner when he does eventually visit the patient: 'He played with my child and gave her a ride on his shoulder, examined all the books on my table, and proved to be a great book-lover and student of philosophy' (*ET* 75, 70). If there is satire in the observation of the doctor's progress from jaunty misdiagnosis of malaria through eventual recognition of typhoid – 'Don't worry. It is a mild attack' (*ET* 77, 72) – to the belated summoning of 'a famous Madras physician' (*ET* 91, 85), Krishnan shows no signs of anger or distrust. He submits equally passively to his mother-in-law's arrangement for the visit of a Hindu holy man to exorcise the Evil Eye. The meticulous maintenance of the sickroom regime in fact produces pleasure rather than anxiety: 'I liked it immensely. It kept me so close to my wife that it produced an immense satisfaction in my mind. Throughout I acted as her nurse. This sickness seemed to bind us together more strongly than ever' (*BA* 81, 76). Only at the moment when the doctor leaves for the last time as Susila is in her death throes, does the style rise from this concentrated attention on the immediate into the rhetoric of an afterlife:

> He turned and walked off. I stood stock still, listening to his shoe creaks going away, the starting of his car; after the car had gone, a stony silence closed in on the house, punctuated by the stentorian breathing, which appeared to me the creaking of the hinges of a prison gate, opening at the command of a soul going into freedom. (*ET* 94, 88)

In some ways the rest of the novel can be taken as a study in bereavement and the struggle to come to terms with it. Krishnan's daughter Leela is crucial in this, as he moves to occupy the role of both mother and father to her. The unheeding aliveness of the little girl shatters the dazed hush of grief. She blows apart the carefully maintained fiction of the mother's continued presence behind the perpetually closed door of the sickroom:

> ... she stole into my room one evening, and whispered, with hardly suppressed glee: 'Father, say what I have done?'
> 'What is it?'
> 'There was no one there and it wasn't locked; so I pushed the door open and went in. Mother is not there!' She shook with suppressed glee, at the thought of her own escapade. (*ET* 102, 97)

Later as she prepares to go to school for the first time, she seems like her mother returned:

> She was ready, dressed in a regalia, and stood before me, a miniature version of her mother. 'Let us go', she said, and for a moment I was unaware whether the mother or the daughter was speaking – the turn of the head and lips! (*ET* 124, 118)

In fact, Krishnan's encounters with Susila through the spiritualist medium can be seen as a sort of back projection of his tender protectiveness towards his daughter on to the lost mother. We notice how much more childlike Susila is in her posthumous state, never any longer the draconian housekeeper reproving her husband for his mistakes in the

31

shopping. It is as though the living daughter and the dead mother coalesce in the tender love/memory of Krishnan.

Yet to read the book only psychologically, with the spiritualistic apparitions no more than the consolatory phantasms of the bereaved, is to evade its full challenge. There is indeed something dreamlike in the way Krishnan receives a mysterious letter from the unknown medium and must follow the boy who brings it to the village outside Malgudi. (In real life, Narayan's encounters with the medium took place in Madras, far away from his home in Mysore where his wife had died.[25]) But the man he meets there, 'a chubby and cheerful-looking person . . . had such good cheer in his face that it melted all the strangeness of the situation' (ET 108, 103). His powers as a medium have come upon him unawares; he is as surprised at the message sent to Krishnan from the afterlife as Krishnan is to receive it. His situation is like a pastoral idyll of retirement: his little farm, garden with lotus-pond and disused temple nearby. And it is in these soothing surroundings that the conditions are right for messages to begin to come through the medium – he is never named – from the dead wife Susila.

The suggestion of idyll, the penumbra of the sacred provided by lotus-pond and temple, may provide a key to the understanding of Krishnan's changed state of mind as he very gradually builds a new relationship with the spirit Susila. It correlates with his other strange encounter in the second half of the book with the 'headmaster' (also nameless) who has set up his own deschooling school in which play is teaching and teaching is play. His school is 'thatch-roofed. Its floor was covered with clay, and the walls were of bamboo splinters filled with mud' (ET 134, 129). He justifies these minimalist surroundings: 'This will do for a school. We are a poor country, and we can do without luxuries. Why do we want anything more than a shed and a few mats and open air?' 'The main business of an educational institution is to shape the mind and character' and all the paraphernalia of government-supported school buildings, the cult of sports, are 'mere copying'. 'It is all a curse, copying, copying, copying. We could as well have been born monkeys to justify our powers of imitation' (ET 135, 129–30). This fits so well with Krishnan's own anti-colonial, anti-educational views that he abandons his job as a college teacher to join the headmaster in his alternative school.

It's not all idyll. There is the grotesque episode in which the headmaster believes he is going to die on a day foretold to him by an astrologer and, when he survives, makes it the occasion for withdrawing himself *sanyasi*-like from his uncomprehending wife, (who has no time for his unorthodox school) and his ragged, ill-cared for children. While the main movement of this part of the book is to take Krishnan to the fulfilment of restored communion with his wife and escape from the drudgery of a career in which he does not believe, it also provokes reflections of philosophic pessimism. When Leela goes away to live with her grandparents – unlike Narayan's own daughter Hema who continued to live with her father in Mysore in a lively joint household with his two married brothers and their families – Krishnan resigns himself to his situation:

> Wife, child, brothers, parents, friends . . . We come together only to go apart again. It is one continuous movement. They move away from us as we move away from them. The law of life can't be avoided. The law comes into operation the moment we detach ourselves from our mother's womb. All struggle and misery in life is due to our attempt to arrest this law or get away from it or in allowing ourselves to be hurt by it. The fact must be recognized. A profound unimitigated loneliness is the only truth of life. (*ET* 177, 171)

At some level, this resigned recognition underlies most of Narayan's fiction, motivating his characters' recurrent need for flight and escape from the trammels of attachment.

In *My Days* Narayan articulates the 'view of personality or self or soul' that developed out of his spiritualist experience.

> 'Now we know in part, then fully, face to face . . .', said St. Paul; our faculties are limited by 'now' and 'here'. . . . Our normal view is limited to a physical perception in a condition restricted in time, like the flashing of a torchlight on a spot, the rest of the area being in darkness. (*MD* 164–5, 144–5)

Behind the Christian teaching of St Paul is the Platonic doctrine of the heavenly Forms of which worldly reality is mere imitation; the nearest Hindu belief would be the concept of *maya*, the phenomenal world as illusion. In *The English Teacher*, uniquely in Narayan, the tragic experience of death forces an attempt to acknowledge this transcendental perspective. More ordinarily the faculties 'limited by 'here' and 'now' represent the pre-condition for the observation of the world of Malgudi, its satisfactions and dissatisfactions, its sensory experience and its constantly mixed skein of emotions. There is a normal acceptance that it can never be other than that; its very materiality is what makes it enjoyable. And yet underlying the rendering of a social world in all its realized specificities and its often bewildered inhabitants is a sense that there *could* be another order of being, another way of living. This is registered in the attempts at escape that so many of the protagonists make but which are always in the end frustrated. It is reflected also in the disproportionate oscillation of moods of ecstasy and despair that so many of them go through all the time. It *might* be otherwise, but not in this life, not in this world. The idyll represented by the relationship with the medium and the headmaster, the perfect communion of Krishnan with his dead wife, the ideal educational system are anti-types to the secular and imperfect world of Malgudi as it really is. It underlines how little Malgudi is in fact the idyll it is often imagined to be. The struggles of its citizens with their intractable problems, domestic, social, political and existential, constitute the imagination of Malgudi and the substance of Narayan's fiction.

2

Politics and Marriage

Narayan in his life and his work took very little interest
in politics. This is the more remarkable in one who lived
in India for the long span he did, through the later phases
of the Raj, the protracted struggle for independence, Partition
and its aftermath, on into the spiralling problems of the
postcolonial state. This lack of political concern has been
the occasion of surprise, criticism, downright condemnation.
H. Y. Sharada Prasad, a student activist in Narayan's own
Maharaja's College in the 1940s and a friend of the writer
who went on to become adviser to three Indian prime
ministers, commented: 'During the Quit India movement
and all when nationalist politics were at fever pitch, Narayan
never issued statements condemning imperialistic perfidy
or the inadequacy of the Cripps Proposals. He appeared
curiously unconcerned and uncommitted'.[1] The photographer
T. S. Satyan, who quotes this statement, though also a close
friend of many years standing, was even more forthright
in his condemnation. Speaking of Narayan's time as a member
of Rajya Sabha, the upper house of the Indian Parliament,
in the 1980s, he called him a 'miserable failure' for never
once raising the problems of his home district of Mysore.[2]
The lack of political concern has been considered by many
as a limitation of Narayan's fiction. So, for instance, V. S.
Naipaul, in an obituary in *Time*, while paying tribute to
his gifts, commented that 'a more clear-sighted man would
not have been able to filter out or make harmless the
distress of India, as Narayan does in Malgudi'.[3] Malgudi
tends to be seen by admirers and critics alike as a protected
zone from which the big issues of politics – the colonial

and postcolonial condition, caste wars, intercommunal violence, the deprivations of poverty – are excluded.

Although such subjects certainly do not figure prominently in the novels, and Malgudi is largely peopled with the middle classes, Narayan was not unaware of a broader spread of society and its political problems. He began his writing career as the Mysore reporter for *The Justice*, a Madras-based daily paper 'intended to promote the cause of the non-Brahmin who suffered from the domination of the minority Brahmin class in public life, government service, and education' (*MD* 123, 108), his own caste notwithstanding. His news-scavenging through the bazaar, law courts and police stations – 'Murders were my stand-by' (*MD* 125, 110) – across the whole district of Mysore not just the city, brought him into contact with a wide variety of lives, rich and poor, officials and village peasants, people of all different classes and castes. This was to provide the raw material for many of his early short stories that chronicle the hardships of the poor, the marginal and the oppressed. But, in spite of this first professional experience, Narayan certainly never became a crusading journalist. When he came to write a fortnightly column for *The Hindu*, he avoided political topics and concentrated on wry observations of everyday social life and manners, only occasionally pursuing a pet grievance such as the attempted imposition of Hindi as first national language on the non-Hindi-speaking south, and the stout defence of the legitimacy of English as a pan-Indian medium.[4] Unlike R. K. Laxman, his younger brother who had acted as his cycle-courier rushing the reports for *The Justice* to the train, and who was to make politics his daily bread as cartoonist for *The Times of India*, Narayan seemed to exclude the whole desperately fraught and contentious area from his work.

Narayan's chosen ground as a writer of fiction is the ordinary, and sometimes extraordinary, domestic and social life within a restricted community affected only indirectly if at all by the larger concerns of the nation. His protagonists are almost always men – young men in pursuit of a wife, or husbands and fathers settled into family life. Yet recurrently in his novels, the foregrounded domestic issues of courtship and marriage provide another way of looking at politics, whether the politics of marriage itself or broader political landscapes within which the personal concerns of the characters are set. Three books in particular, from early, middle and later periods of Narayan's career, can be used to illustrate this underpinning of the domestic by the political. *The Dark Room* (1938), with its unique woman central character and its avowedly feminist focus, analyses the power dynamics of an Indian middle-class marriage. *Waiting for the Mahatma* (1955) places Sriram's pursuit of his adored Bharati against the backdrop of the crucial culminating years of India's movement toward Independence. And *The Painter of Signs* (1976), written during the Emergency, makes the highly topical issue of birth control the centre of contention between the lovers Raman and Daisy. These are not novel about politics, nor in the normal sense politically engaged; but in their own distinctive way they reflect and mediate key political issues.

WRITING BACK TO IBSEN

The Dark Room (1938) has a narrative shape familiar from many other Narayan novels. The first phase of the book establishes the situation, the rhythms of an accustomed life; with the arrival of a newcomer, there is a crisis, precipitating the flight from home of the central figure; after a time in a religious life seeking to shed normal social and personal identity, the protagonist returns to the ordinary world of the beginning. It is a pattern already more or less there in *Swami and Friends* and *The Bachelor of Arts*. What makes this, Narayan's third novel, so different from the autobiographical trilogy looked at in the previous chapter, is its focus on a female character and the explicitness of its concern with issues of gender. About the latter, Narayan seemed uneasily self-conscious when looking back at the book in his autobiography at a distance of more than thirty-five years:

> I was somehow obsessed with a philosophy of Woman as opposed to Man, her constant oppressor. This must have been an early testament of the 'Women's Lib' movement. Man assigned her a secondary place and kept her there with such subtlety and cunning that she herself began to lose all notion of her independence, her individuality, stature, and strength. (*MD* 132, 115–16)

37

Writing in the 1970s, Narayan here sees the novel as a forerunner of the women's movement that had gathered momentum by that time. But he might equally have claimed the book as an Indian response to one of the great landmark works of European feminism, Ibsen's *A Doll's House*.[5] From its first publication in 1879 and the many productions that followed, the drama of Nora Helmer's rejection of her doll's house role as wife and mother caused intense controversy; her bold renunciation of her duties as wife and mother became a key challenge to patriarchy. *The Dark Room*, which (whether consciously or not) reproduces some of the key features of Ibsen's play, can be read as a demonstration of the bleaker situation of the Indian wife that makes impossible any such liberationary outcome as Nora's slamming of the doll's house door.

Savitri is a wife and mother like Nora, both of them with three children. Narayan the novelist immerses us in Savitri's maternal concern from the opening line: 'At schooltime Babu suddenly felt very ill, and Savitri fussed over him and put him to bed' (*DR* 1, 1). Nora's children are not Ibsen's main concern, and he sensibly keeps them off stage most of the time. By contrast Savitri's is no doll's house play role but the demanding task of coping with household, servants, children and a domineering husband whose every whim must be humoured. This normal continuum is contrasted early in the novel with the special festival time of Navaratri, when a whole array of traditional dolls are taken out of storage and the mother, family and family servant can temporarily share a magical other world. The magic is shattered, however, when one of the dolls is broken, the young son Babu's attempt to rig up spectacular lighting effects goes awry, and the father punishes him with disproportionate anger. It is this that sends Savitri into her one refuge at times of extreme stress, the dark room. The western woman may aspire to a room of her own as token of her independence; for this intolerably bullied Indian wife there is only withdrawal into silence and self-starvation in the dark space behind the kitchen store.

She is eventually coaxed out by her older friend Janamma who holds to the orthodox principle that a woman must submit to her husband in all things. But the incident sets up the recurrent impulse of despair in Savitri which drives her towards the darkness of non-being. In *A Doll's House* Ibsen provides an elaborate plot mechanism that takes Nora to the point of suicide. In order to borrow money to save her husband's life when he was dangerously ill, she forged a signature not knowing it to be illegal and, under the threat of exposure, she decides to kill herself in order to save her husband from (as she thinks) nobly shouldering the blame. In place of this melodramatic chain of events, culminating in Nora's frenetic dancing of the tarantella as she prepares to die, Savitri's crisis is much more straightforwardly occasioned by her husband's infidelity; Ramani has started an affair with a trainee in his office, the flirtatious Shanta Bai who plays on her position as independent divorcée. And where Ibsen's denouement gives to Nora a conversion experience in which she can declare her separation from Helmer, Savitri's confrontation with her husband moves her to a despairing awareness of her complete material dependence: 'What possession can a woman call her own except her body? Everything else that she has is her father's, her husband's, or her son's'. She even accepts Ramani's assertion that the children are his: 'Yes, you are right. They are yours, absolutely. You paid the midwife and the nurse. You pay for their clothes and teachers. You are right. Didn't I say that a woman owns nothing?' (*DR* 88, 113).

In flight from the family home and these properties to which she can claim no ownership, Savitri reflects bitterly on woman's dependence on her sexuality:

> What is the difference between a prostitute and a married woman? – the prostitute changes her men, but a married woman doesn't; that's all, but both earn their food and shelter in the same manner. (*DR* 93, 120)

This is close to the fierce polemics of Shaw's *Mrs Warren's Profession* (1893), for so many years banned on the British stage because of its scandalous equation of bourgeois marriage with prostitution. Certainly in the novel we see Savitri's perception borne out by the way in which her rival Shanta Bai, excluded from respectably married status, manipulates her sexual attractions with her boss Ramani. 'No one who couldn't live by herself had a right to exist' (*DR* 94, 120), this is Savitri's conclusion. It is under the pressure of this logic, even though uncertain to the last, that she prepares to drown herself in the river Sarayu, going to death as the darkest space of all.

Savitri is rescued by the blacksmith-cum-burglar Mari, and the second half of the novel shows just how impossible it is for the Indian middle-class woman to 'live by herself'. Almost hysterically determined not to accept charity, she refuses the food and drink offered her by Mari and Ponni, his very bossy but kindly wife. They can only assume this is because, as she is a Brahmin, any food they prepare would be contaminated by their low-caste status. Ponni negotiates a job for her with the miserly and cantankerous priest of the local temple – Hindu priests in Narayan are quite often portrayed as figures neither unworldly nor benign. For miserable pay and the barest of subsistence food, Savitri is to be cleaner and maid-of-all-work in the temple. At first she is triumphant to be earning her own living, however poor. But a single terrifying night in the shanty adjoining the temple, which is her dark room accommodation, and yearning thoughts of her children drive her back to the family home. We see no conclusive evidence after her return that she will be able to act on Ponni's tough-minded advice: 'Remember; men are good creatures, but you must never give way to them. Be firm and they will behave' (*DR* 148, 192).

The Dark Room thus may appear a bitter demonstration that, while for the Norwegian Nora Helmer separation from the family and a positive declaration of the sovereignty of the self may be possible, no such option is available for an Indian Savitri. However, the politics of Narayan's novel involve issues of class as well as gender. From the beginning of the book, we are made more than usually aware of the servants in the middle-class family home. Ranga, the general 'hey-you' round the house, clowns for the children as he lays out the Navaratri dolls, but when he breaks one of them, the young daughter Kamala reacts immediately: 'Make him buy a new one, Mother. Don't give him his pay' (*DR* 29, 35). And even in its broken state, though they have five hundred other such dolls, Kamala will not let Ranga take it home for his little boy. When Ramani orders a space in the office to be cleared for Shanta Bai to live in, 'the old office watchman resented it because the passage room had been for years his home' (*DR* 53, 69). It is shocking to see how the put-upon Savitri takes out her unhappiness on the maidservant, 'an old woman who had done a few years service in the house' (*DR* 74, 95):

> 'Why do you shout at me, my lady? What have I done?'
> 'I will shout as I please. You are not the person to question me. If you don't like it, you had better go out'.   (*DR* 73, 94)

Savitri is at the mercy of her bullying husband, but the working underclasses are just as subject to the arbitrary tyranny of their bourgeois employers, male and female.

Narayan enforces the point about the gap between the classes by a shift in focus halfway through the book. He ends Chapter 7 with the apparent suicide of Savitri. Chapter 8 starts a new narrative arc, which will of course end with Savitri's rescue:

> Burglary was only a side occupation of Mari. He was the locksmith, unbrella-repairer, and blacksmith of Sukkur village, which was a couple of miles from the other bank of the river.   (*DR* 95, 122)

What follows takes us through a day in the life of such a person. We see Mari struggling to find work, walking the streets of Malgudi, offering his services repairing umbrellas or mending locks. His total income for the day is six pies, which after much haggling with a street vendor, he spends on some groundnut and fried stuff, with a slice of cucumber, cucumber which we have heard the cranky Ramani describe as 'the cheapest trash in the market' (*DR* 2, 3). Narayan points up the enormous gap between the earning power of the comfortable middle class and the working tradesman. Ramani, a self-made man who has obstinately refused to follow his father's advice and go to college, is proud of his position as head of the local insurance company office, with an income of 'a clear five hundred a month, in salary alone' (*DR* 109, 140). He casually throws out a rupee to his wife to buy vegetables for the evening meal. Mari can only fantasize about a time when he earned a whole rupee in a day. The pie was the smallest unit of Indian currency, with 192 pies to the rupee, so the six pies

Mari takes in and spends on food is a tiny fraction of the disposable income of Ramani. It is no wonder Mari targets an empty house in the affluent Lawley Extension for burglary, and hungrily eats the crust of three-day-old bread that is all the holidaying family has left behind in it.

Savitri's brief stay in the village where Mari and Ponni live further illustrates the huge differences between the way the rich and poor live. The strong-minded Ponni manages to take a bunch of plantains and a coconut on credit from the local shopkeeper, as the only food she thinks the Brahmin Savitri will take from her. In order to persuade the miserly priest to give Savitri a job, Mari has to agree to mend a whole heap of broken tools, 'two days of profitless labour' (*DR* 128, 166). In the context of these socio-economic realities, Savitri's despairing rejection of her home begins to seem like a freak of middle-class hysteria. There is no lack of sympathy for her plight but a full awareness of the power dynamics of the society as a whole. Savitri is elated by the thought that she can devote her life to the service of the god. In fact, she will be the servant of a callous and contemptuous priest, a master considerably more brutal than her autocratic husband. There is no female equivalent of the *sanyasi*, the man who is revered for his renunciation of the world, the role temporarily adopted by Chandran in *The Bachelor of Arts*. Even in this the woman is disadvantaged in Indian society.

The Dark Room is a book about power dynamics – the complete power of man over woman in the middle-class marriage, but the power also of caste, class and money over those at the bottom of the system. In this too it speaks back to *A Doll's House* in which the emancipation of Nora can be seen to be based in a purely bourgeois individualism. There is a bitter little afterpiece to *The Dark Room* that reinforces its class message. Savitri, some days after her restoration to the comforts of home and family, hears the voice of Mari offering his services in the street. Her first impulse is to invite him in: 'She could give him food, water, and a magnificent gift, and inquire about her great friend Ponni; perhaps Ponni had sent him along now' (*DR* 161, 209). But this impulse is soon checked; the class barriers are back in place, and she lets Mari pass unacknowledged. The book ends with her sense of betrayal: 'She sat by the window, haunted by his shining hungry face long after he was gone, and by his "Locks repaired . . ." long after his cry had faded out in the distance' (*DR* 162, 210).

It is a pointed ending such as Narayan never used in any other of his novels; his characteristic technique is the anti-climactic inconclusive conclusion. But then *The Dark Room* is a novel unlike any other that he wrote, and some of the problems of the book may suggest why he did not repeat the experiment. As often happens where a middle-class novelist writes with good political intentions towards the working class, there is a tendency towards condescending idealization. Narayan is close to sentimentality with the portrait of Ponni, the tough-minded termagant with a kindly heart, and her relationship with her hen-pecked husband Mari so comically unlike the marriage of Savitri and Ramani. The ending has a clanging obviousness that brings out by contrast the sublety of Narayan's normal style. The situation of Savitri is rendered with force and feeling, but there is in the end a certain thinness of characterization that may relate to the book's tendentious theme. For whatever reason, Narayan chose never to repeat this anatomy of a bad marriage from the woman's point of view or to tackle social issues of class so directly. In later books the novelist reverts to a male protagonist, obsessed with marrying a woman whose inde-pendence of spirit and political commitments remain for him a bewildering mystery.

SLEEPWALKING THROUGH HISTORY

Narayan's early novels are not without some awareness of contemporary political events and their impact. In *Swami and Friends* we see Swami carried away by the rhetoric of a Gandhian leader at a protest meeting in 1930, as Narayan himself, at an equivalent age joined 'the first nationalist agitation in Madras, in 1916'. The young Narayan was scolded by his 'anti-political' uncle, who 'condemned all rulers, gov-ernments and administrative machinery as Satanic and saw no logic in seeking a change of rulers' (*MD* 14, 13). In the novel

Swami is swept up in the group feeling, exulting in breaking the school windows, brow-beaten into throwing his 'foreign' (i.e. non-Indian-made) cap into the bonfire as part of the Gandhian principle of wearing only home-produced clothes. In the aftermath, Swami is expelled from the Albert Mission School in spite of his best efforts to deny his involvement, and is mortified to discover that his cap had been a properly nationalist 'khaddar cap' bought by his father who 'won't have a paisa of mine sent to foreign countries'. 'Why do not you urchins leave politics alone and mind your business?', the father says crossly (SF 103). Something of his uncle's anarchist distrust of all forms of organized government and bureaucracy, together with a horror of group violence shown most vividly in his angry story 'Another Community' set during the 1947 Partition riots (UBT 67–72), underlies Narayan's distanced attitude towards political movements in his fiction.

Once again, the contrast with the other two landmark Indian novels of the period points the difference. Kanthapura is a wholeheartedly Gandhian novel, showing the small village community as a paradigm for the country as a whole; Gandhi's local avatar, Moorthy, by his combination of Brahmin piety and political fervour, succeeds in welding solidarity between castes and creeds in the freedom struggle. Anand's socialism in Untouchable will not allow him such unqualified assent to the Gandhian principles, but an appearance by Gandhi himself and his message of the evils of untouchability provide a clinching climax to the action. Political feeling in Narayan is never exemplary as it is in Rao and Anand, and rarely fully ardent and committed. Much more typical is the train of thought that runs through Chandran's mind in The Bachelor of Arts as he watches the English Principal of the Albert Mission College chair a debate:

> Here he is, Chandran thought, pretending to press the bell and listen to the speeches, but really his thoughts are at the tennis-court and the card-table in the English Club. He is here not out of love for us, but merely to keep up appearances. All Europeans are like this. . . . Why should not these fellows admit Indians to their clubs? Sheer colour arrogance. If ever I get into power I shall see that Englishmen attend clubs along with Indians and are not so exclusive.

So far so predictable – the young Indian's understandable resentment of imperial racist domination. But then there is an unexpected double jump of feeling:

> Why not give the poor devils – so far away from their home – a chance to club together at least for a few hours at the end of a day's work? Anyway who invited them here? (*BA* 5, 19–20)

The momentary surge of imaginative empathy is followed by an even more petulant backwash of anger. In Narayan, any sustained political commitment is liable to be swayed by the instability of such micromoods of emotion.

Indian novelists in English, like so many other postcolonial writers, have tended to be preoccupied, not to say obsessed with their own history. *Midnight's Children* (1981) is only the most famous and the most self-conscious example of the fiction that tracks, refracts or exemplifies the national narrative of events. From *Kanthapura*, set at the time of Gandhi's Salt March, through Kushwant Singh's *Train to Pakistan* (1956), one of innumerable Partition novels, through to Aravind Adiga's *Between the Assassinations* (2008) – those of Indira and Rahjiv Gandhi – this has been a staple form. Narayan only once attempted such a book, in *Waiting for the Mahatma*. The action of this novel follows through the sequence of Indian history from 1941 to 1948, and it shows the personal impact of Gandhi who appears as one of the characters. Yet the narrative remains curiously dislocated from the history against which it is set by virtue of the only partially comprehending perspective of the central character.

A naïve lack of understanding and engagement is character-istic of many of Narayan's male protagonists; William Walsh borrows D. H. Lawrence's phrase 'a peculiar, nuclear inno-cence' to describe it.[6] But among such figures Sriram is quite exceptionally estranged from his surroundings. He is an orphan, living alone with his grandmother, who reaches the age of twenty without apparently having made any friends or connections outside the home. Coming into his inheritance, the accumulated British army pension owing to him because his father was killed in the First World War, he can think of nothing better to do but sit in his chair all day and watch the street outside. He is only jolted into life one day in the market when an attractive young woman asks him for a contribution for her collecting box. He has no idea what she is collecting for; all he wants to ask is, 'How old are you? What caste are you? Where is your horoscope? Are you free to marry me?' (*WM* 22). It takes him some time to discover that she is a Congress worker and that her appearance in Malgudi heralds that of the Mahatma himself: 'Sriram suddenly woke from an age-old somnolence to the fact that Malgudi was about to have the honour of receiving Mahatma Gandhi' (*WM* 24).

The 'age-old somnolence', the all but autistic state of mind of Sriram, are clues to a fable-like design to the novel. The young woman is called Bharati, so named by Gandhi himself: 'Bharat is India, and Bharati is the daughter of India' (*WM* 59). While Sriram's father died fighting for the British in Mesopotamia, her father was killed in the freedom movement in 1920. The unawakened ordinary young Indian, product of orthodox Brahminism and an unthinking acceptance of the Raj, is awakened by Bharati to the new vision of his country. His marriage to her, constantly deferred until the Mahatma feels the time is right to give them his blessing, will represent the harmonious fusion of the old and the new. Certainly the role of the grandmother, pillar of orthodoxy that she is, has a suggestion of the allegorical. Gandhi demands that Sriram obtain his grandmother's blessing before committing himself to the dedicated life of a volunteer, something he is too cowardly to do. Much later in the book, he comes out of hiding to attend her funeral only to see her corpse stir back into life. The resurrection of the supposedly dead old woman is emblematic of the indestructible vitality of the traditional in India for all its changes. 'India will go on', as Narayan famously told V. S. Naipaul.[7]

And yet there is much in the book that works against any such schematic reading of it as allegory.[8] Narayan's comic observation of the social context checks and thwarts any abstract interpretative pattern. The occasion of Gandhi's visit, for instance, elicits a cool satire on Maguldi officialdom. In the Reception Committee, the Municipal Chairman negotiates to have the honour of accommodating the Mahatma in his own palatial residence. The British Collector silkily plays his diplomatic part, even though everyone present knows that if he chose 'he could close the entire meeting and put all the members behind bars under the Defence of India Act' (*WM* 39). On the day of Gandhi's arrival, the Chairman proudly leads him to his grand mansion where every luxury has been laid on. He is taken aback at the invasion of followers that this brings, and appalled when Gandhi installs beside himself on the sofa of honour the filthiest of the sweeper boys from the crowd. He is even more horrified when the Mahatma chooses to follow the boy to the disreputable sweepers' slum and stay in one of the huts there rather than in the Chairman's specially prepared residence. An instant beautification of the colony hastily follows, at which Gandhi slyly remarks, 'Now one can believe that the true cleansers of the city live here' (*WM* 52). Malgudi is not miraculously transformed by the impact of the Gandhian message as Rao's Kanthapura was, but struggles to cope with the unpredictable phenomenon of the Mahatma.

Wedged among the huge crowds assembled to hear Gandhi speak under a broiling sun, Sriram reflects 'Waiting for the Mahatma makes one very thirsty' (*WM* 25). This first mention of the book's title gives it an ironic edge. Sriram's conversion to Gandhianism is materially embedded, and animated by his infatuated pursuit of the unknown Bharati. Though he joins the camp of volunteers, and with infinite effort learns to spin the yarn for his own clothes, he never really understands the principles of commitment by which his beloved lives. Acting on the instructions of the Mahatma, delivered by Bharati, who has been constituted his guru, Sriram is established on his own in a 'deserted shrine on a slope of the Mempi Hill' (*WM* 94). It is the summer of 1942, when Gandhi has launched the 'Quit India' campaign, and Sriram's mission is to paint up the slogan on every available wall space. The letter 'Q' with its long tail seems to involve unnecessary amounts of black paint, so for economy's sake, the message comes out as 'Ouit India' (*WR* 103). We are given glimpses of other discouraging setbacks in Sriram's mission, such as his farcical attempt to prevent a village shopman from selling British biscuits, or his disconcertingly friendly reception by the planter Mathieson, who tries to engage him in polite political discussion. 'Don't you think it is a pity you should have turned down Cripps's offer?' he asks Sriram, alluding to the British delegation in March 1942 led by

Sir Stafford Cripps that had proposed full Dominion status for India in exchange for support of the war effort. To Sriram, this was 'a technical point with which he was not concerned. Such intricate academic technicalities refused to enter his head, and so he merely said, "Mahatmaji does not think so", and there was an end to the discussion' (*WM* 113).

Incidents such as this reflect what one critic sees as 'colonial ambivalence' in the novel, a residual allegiance to the imperial status quo shadowing Narayan's depiction of the freedom movement.[9] But it is hard to be sure just what Sriram's erratic career as a freedom fighter does represent. He fails to go voluntarily to prison as Bharati does, acting on Gandhi's instructions. With Bharati absent, he comes under the influence of the sinisterly comic photographer Jagadish, who enlists him as propagandist and saboteur on behalf of the militant Indian National Army under the leadership of Subhas Chandra Bhose, a manifest betrayal of his Gandhian principles. Coming out of hiding to attend the funeral of his – as it turns out – undead grandmother, he is arrested and imprisoned. Because he is not classed as a political prisoner, he is not released under amnesty with the other Gandhians and arrives belatedly like an awakened Rip Van Winkle into a fully independent India. He returns to his pursuit of Bharati and is at last reunited with her in Delhi, where she is working with Gandhi in the refugee campaigns set up in the wake of Partition. The long-deferred consummation seems at hand, and sure enough, Gandhi gives his blessing and promises to marry them himself the following day. However, the setting of Birla House and the date of January 1948 will alert any reader with the slightest knowledge of Indian history to what is coming. These are the last lines of the book: 'As the Mahatma was about to step on the dais, the man took aim and fired. Two more shots rang out. The Mahatma fell on the dais. He was dead in a few seconds' (*WM* 254).

The appearances of Gandhi in the book give a sense of the force of his personality: his spiritual devotion, his kindly directness, his prodigious energy and capacity for multi-tasking, the impact of his austere integrity on everyone who meets him. What is more, we are given glimpses at least of the traumas that afflicted India in the period. The Mahatma tours famine-afflicted areas in the vicinity of Malgudi, a reminder of the terrible famine that devastated Bengal in 1943. Sriram, whose idea of the village is based on the idyllic sterotypes of Tamil films is astonished by what he sees: 'Hungry, parched men and women with skin stretched over their bones, bare earth, dry ponds, and miserable tattered thatched roofing over crumbling mud walls, streets full of pits and loose sand, unattractive dry fields – that was a village' (*WM* 89). While others were celebrating Independence, Bharati tells how she followed Gandhi on his barefoot mission through East Bengal torn apart by the Partition riots. 'We stopped for a day or two in each village, and he spoke to those who had lost their homes, property, wives and children. He spoke kindly to those who had perpetrated crimes – he wept for them'. There could be no taking sides between one community and another: 'Human beings have done impossible things to other human beings' (*WM* 244). Such was the heartbreaking conclusion to Gandhi's career-long vision of a free, peaceful, united India where all castes and creeds were equally respected.

In *Waiting for the Mahatma*, however, we see all this through the myopically blinkered vision of one of Narayan's mooniest anti-heroes. Sriram never fully awakes from his 'age-old somnolence' but sleepwalks through history. Throughout all the varied phases of his involvement in the freedom movement and the deprivations of prison life, Sriram remains concentrated on just one object, union with the woman whose committed politics he does not half understand. Even in the Delhi refugee camp, peopled by the many orphans who are Bharati's special care, he fondles her sari in her absence, fantasizes about the domesticity they will share. It is hard for a reader not to feel some impatience, as Bharati herself does, with the triviality of this sort of personal romancing in the context of the surroundings. The long awaited happy ending is guaranteed to the couple finally; Gandhi, visited by a premonition that he will not be there to act as their priest the following day, orders them 'not to put off your marriage for any reason' (*WM* 253). But this traditional comic conclusion is overtaken by the shocking tragedy of Gandhi's assassination. If Sriram stands for some sort of ordinary man, his inability to conceive any goal in life but marriage and happy-ever-after matches India's larger historic failure to meet the challenge of Gandhi's Utopian vision.

LOVE IN THE 1970s

The plot of *The Painter of Signs* is practically a re-run of *Waiting for the Mahatma*; gentle unattached young man pursues independent young woman with a view to marriage. But the novel is set a generation later, and as the young man Raman reflects, cycling through the traffic, 'Malgudi was changing in 1972. It was the base for a hydroelectric project somewhere on the Mempi Hills, and jeeps and lorries passed through the Market Road all day' (*PS* 12, 13–14). Gandhi is now a revered figure of the past, his face a standard icon that appears on Raman's tool-bag. The Prime Minister of the time is the totally unrelated Indira Gandhi, daughter of Nehru, who in 1975 was to declare the Emergency and rule unconstitutionally until 1977. *The Painter of Signs*, though the action was antedated by a few years, was in fact written during the Emergency and published in 1976. That made it a very topical book, at least in so far as the mission of the independent young woman Daisy is to advance the cause of family planning in India, and one of the most notorious features of Indira Gandhi's Emergency regime was the campaign of sterilization organized by her son Sanjay. Narayan himself, normally so reluctant to associate his work with politics, in a retrospective interview years later, admitted that *The Painter of Signs* was linked to 'a time when thousands had been coerced into sometimes fatal sterilizing operations'.[10] What is the effect of Narayan's story of the relationship of Raman and Daisy within this contemporary political context, and in what ways does it differ from the comparable relationship in *Waiting for the Mahatma*?

By setting the book back in time, Narayan avoids making it an Emergency novel; there is certainly none of the sense of political anger against Gandhi's regime that fires *Midnight's Children* or Rohinton Mistry's *A Fine Balance*. The Prime Minister's name is in fact only mentioned once in passing, and that can be discounted because of the speaker, the coffee-house talker Gupta 'who was always incensed over government politics' (*PS* 15, 16). John Thieme suggests that Narayan may have soft-pedalled any criticism of Gandhi in the book because of his 'very real respect for this member of post-Independence India's most renowned family' (Thieme 138). Against that there is the article Narayan wrote in the immediate aftermath of the Emergency, celebrating the end of press censorship when 'the average citizen was convinced that day by day he was being fed on exaggeration, half-truths, quarter-truths and mini-truths, if not lies' (*Writerly Life* 435). *The Painter of Signs* is not a polemic political novel, but in its dramatization of the troubled love of Raman for Daisy it reaches out to some of the underlying social and cultural issues of postcolonial India.

Their relationship has none of the fable-like quality of Sriram and Bharati in *Waiting for the Mahatma*. Raman is solidly characterized, university educated, an omnivorous reader who has chosen his profession as sign-painter, which he regards as an art-form, because of his appreciation of calligraphy. He is a bachelor of thirty, who has deliberately avoided marriage, choosing to live instead with his devout old aunt, whose often repeated pious anecdotes he only half hears. There is no love at first sight encounter with Daisy, but a gradually developing obsession with the woman who hires him initially to paint a sign for her family planning clinic, subsequently to accompany her through the surrounding countryside to put up signs promoting birth control. She also is no semi-allegorical Bharati figure. She appears with the untraceably unIndian name of Daisy – '*That* girl', Raman's aunt exclaims with horror when he eventually tells her they are going to marry, 'What is her caste? Who is she?' (*PS* 146, 115). However, in the course of the book we learn her backstory, as a girl who grew up in a conventional Indian joint family but revolted against an arranged marriage, ran away, and with the help of a Christian missionary, re-made herself as Daisy, earnest advocate of birth control.

Raman prides himself on his rationalism. 'All day long he was engaged in arguing with his old aunt who advised him to do this or that according to the stars. He was determined to establish the Age of Reason in the world' (*PS* 5, 8). Anti-traditionalist though he may be, he is unprepared for the uncompromising materialism of Daisy, who speaks 'without the slightest inhibition, about the course a recalcitrant sperm took and the strategy to halt its journey' (*PS* 87, 70). He finds himself, as one critic puts it, 'sandwiched between Malgudi's conventions and the Outsider's iconoclasm, between the philosophies of the Traditional Woman (his aunt) and the New Woman (Daisy)'.[11] The strength of the novel lies in the delicate comedy that Narayan creates out of Raman's situation, while never slighting the seriousness and depth of what underlies it.

The problem of overpopulation is something that even Raman has noticed, though he tries to shrug it off: 'The town hall veranda and the pavements around the market, the no-man's lands of Malgudi, swarmed with children of all sizes, from toddlers to four-footers, dust-covered, ragged – a visible development in five years. At this rate, they would overrun the globe – no harm; though they looked famished, their brown or dark skin shone with health and their liquid eyes sparkled with life' (*PS* 30, 27). There can be no such aestheticizing of poverty for Daisy. When a village school teacher is inclined to feel that the evil of unchecked population growth has been exaggerated, she relentlessly demonstrates the economic facts: the population of his village has increased by twenty per cent in the previous year – 'Has your food production increased twenty per cent? Have your accommodations increased twenty per cent? I know they haven't'. Against such implacable logic, Raman's reaction is absurdly wrong-headed: 'She must be really mad! She will fight and shun people who bring up large families. Some madness must have got into her head quite early in life and stayed on there' (*PS* 67, 55).

The book commands real respect for Daisy and her single-minded crusade to educate the people in family planning. Her principles are high-minded and entirely ethical. She explains gently to the villager whose wife is pregnant for the tenth time in twelve years that she does not perform abortions. She rejects indignantly the proposal of the bangle-seller in the market to supply bangles for the women to induce them to have sterilization operations: 'We don't believe in that kind of conversion. They must understand what they are doing, and not be enticed in this childish manner' (*PS* 143, 113). She is thus distanced from the real-life practices of Sanjay Gandhi's infamous campaign, where transistor radios were given out to those willing to undergo vasectomies. Still, there are forces resisting Daisy's enlightened belief in family planning other than the ill-educated backwardness of the people. This is represented in the strange episode where she is confronted by a village hermit, the only point in the book where we see Daisy daunted. The hermit presides over a shrine to the Goddess of Plenty guaranteed to bring conception to barren women who pray there, and thus, as Daisy herself realizes, 'the antithesis of all her mission' (*PS* 70, 58). He denounces his antagonist: 'Be careful, you evil woman, don't tamper with God's designs. He will strike you dead if you attempt that' (*PS* 71, 58). There is no sign of Daisy being struck dead in the novel, but the priest's authority here is increased by his yogi-like capacity to reveal the secrets of her past life. He stands for an atavistic power unyielding before the beliefs of modern rational enlightenment.

The sexual comedy of Raman's pursuit of Daisy is made funnier and deeper by the very fact that her mission in life is to control sexual reproduction. Raman, as apostle of Reason, has self-consciously tried to discipline his own urges; that is one of the reasons that he has decided not to marry. He reproaches himself with his inability to keep his mind off Daisy – 'I'm sex-obsessed, that's all, to admit the plain fact' (*PS* 39, 34). He moralizes on the reductiveness of his own male gaze: 'That is the tragedy of womanhood – utility articles whether in bed or not' (*PS* 46, 39). This only makes the more endearing Raman's inevitable fall into lovesickness – more endearing and more credible than the blank besottedness of Sriram for Bharati in *Waiting for the Mahatma*. The climax of this comedy comes when Raman and Daisy find themselves alone together on a long bullock-cart journey back to Malgudi from one of the more remote villages. The cart driver is an old-fashioned enthusiast for married life, currently on to his fifth wife, having had four children with each of the previous four: 'God gives us children, and who are we to say no to Him?' (*PS* 83, 67). He treats Raman and Daisy with jocular encouragement as a newly-married couple, though the only courtship gambit Raman can think of is to get Daisy to expatiate on contraception. When one of the bullocks goes lame, and the cart driver has to go off to look for a replacement, Raman takes advantage of being alone with his beloved to attempt seduction, rape if necessary, only to discover that Daisy has easily outmanoeuvred him by taking refuge up a tree.

Romantic comedy has marriage and sexual union as its traditional conclusion, however little the course of true love may have run smoothly along the way. *The Painter of Signs* looks as though it is going to conform to this traditional pattern. After a period of estrangement following the night on the bullock-cart (when Raman is terrified he is about to be arrested for attempted rape), Daisy softens towards him and they consummate their love. She agrees to marry, if only according to the least binding 'Gandharva-style marriage, as easily snapped as made' (*PS* 169, 132), and on her own terms: no children and no interference with her career. The marriage plans precipitate the departure of Raman's aunt on a pilgrimage to Benares where she plans to end her life. It is only at this point that Raman realizes how much he will miss the pious old woman, how reliant he has been on the dependable familiarity of her devoutness and devotion to himself. Nonetheless, the way is cleared for marriage between Daisy and Raman, the Brahmin man united with the progressive modern woman.

Only it does not happen. At the last moment, an urgent call to work in a remote part of the country where she is needed makes Daisy decide against going on with the marriage to Raman. 'Married life', she tells him, 'is not for me. I have thought it over. It frightens me. I am not cut out for the life you imagine. I can't live except alone. It won't work' (*PS* 178–9, 139). Raman is distraught, tries to argue her out of her decision, promise at least to return, but she is resolute. In the coda to the novel, he is left desolate at losing her, yet at some level reassured to be freed from the disturbance that she represented, free to go back to the accustomed homosocial company of men at the Boardless café (so-called for its lack of a signboard):

> He reflected, Maybe we will live together in our next Janma [birth]. At least then she will leave people alone, I hope. . . . He mounted his cycle and turned towards The Boardless – that solid, real world of sublime souls who minded their own business. (*PS* 183, 143)

It is a beautifully ironic ending, the irony exposing the inadequacy of Raman's attraction to Daisy, the inertia that takes him back to the contented bachelordom of the beginning. This sort of return to normality, so common in Narayan, is often regarded as a reflection of his resistance to political change, but it is not necessarily so. Lakshmi Holmström sums up helpfully the role of women as markers of social change in three of the novels, *The Guide* as well as *The Dark Room* and *The Painter of Signs*:

> Some of the women characters are symbols of a particular kind of social change, struggling to redefine themselves as women: unique and lonely figures. At the same time, they are presented from the outside, often through the perspective of not entirely reliable narrrators. As such, the ambiguity of their presentation mirrors . . . the bafflement of a conservative society face to face with what is deeply subversive of it; perhaps the honest bafflement of the author, too.[12]

This is well said. It may be added that the novels that register the impact of such women through unreliable male narrators are more effective than *The Dark Room*, Narayan's one attempt to confront the political issue of gender directly from the woman's point of view. It is the very fogginess of Sriram and Raman's perspective, the inadequacy of the idea of marriage that drives them on, and their incapacity to understand the larger issues of national politics and social problems that motivate the women they love, that make these books something much more than the mild romantic comedies they appear to be.

3

Embedded Myths

MYTHIC FORM

Homi Bhabha, reviewing *The Painter of Signs* when it first appeared, called it 'a contemporary reading between the lines of a classical Indian epic'. Daisy, he affirmed, is a modern counterpart of 'an antique goddess, the wife of King Santhanu'.

> The daughter of Jahnu, the goddess married Santhanu on the same condition that Daisy married Raman – that he should never cross her will. The goddess only marries the king to accomplish the purpose of the gods. Raman's wife, like Santhanu's, acts not in life or for it; both fulfil a need that is implicitly against it. The only difference is that the former prevents children, the latter kills seven of her own.[1]

Raman in the novel actually identifies himself with Santhanu in the absoluteness of his submission to Daisy (*PS* 159, 125). The story is the one with which Narayan begins his re-telling of the *Mahabharata*: Santhanu's wife is in fact Ganga, the deity of the river; the king drowns seven of their children at her bidding, but the eighth will survive to become Bhishma, one of the central figures of the epic (*Mahabharata* 1–3). But how far and in what way can the story of Santhanu, so incidentally mentioned by Raman, be read into *The Painter of Signs*? The question is related to the much broader issue of Narayan's use of material from Hindu mythology and legend within his fiction. Two other examples from *The Dark Room* may help to illustrate the problem. The central character in the novel is called Savitri, a figure from one of the incidental stories in the *Mahabharata*, re-told in Narayan's collection *Gods, Demons and*

56

Others (182–9), who is a model of wifely self-sacrifice, prepared to do anything to save her husband from death. John Thieme in fact suggests that the novel might be seen as 'a reworking of the mythic archetype of Savitri' (Thieme 47). The 'dark room' of the novel's title might also have an epic source, this time from the *Ramayana*; it could be identified with the *kopa gruha*, 'the room of anger, which was a part of a dwelling where one could retire to work off a bad mood' (*Ramayana* 43), which Queen Kaikeyi uses to manipulate her husband Dasaratha to prevent the coronation of her stepson Rama. Is there active irony in these glancing epic echoes, given that the latter-day Savitri achieves so little from her self-sacrifice, is so unsuccessful in her use of the retreat to the dark room?

Meenakshi Muhkerjee in *The Twice Born Fiction*, her influential study of Indian novels in English, commented on how, in contrast to the use of myth in the West which became a standard feature of modernism from *Ulysses* on, 'the consciousness of myth was very slow to evolve in Indo-Anglian fiction'.[2] That book was published in 1971, and since *Midnight's Children* (1981) modernist and post-modernist play with mythic narratives and motifs has become common in the Indian novel. Still Mukherjee's observation is striking in relation to Narayan and his contemporaries. It may well be that, as she suggests, 'too close a proximity of the writer to these myths' may have contributed to this late development.[3] At least, novelists in a society where Hindu legendary narratives remained current, regularly re-cycled in Bollywood movies (as they are in *Mr Sampath*), may have felt less need for a self-conscious recovery of mythic archetypes as the structuring principle of literary fiction. In reading *Ulysses* we must dig below the events of the 1904 day in the life of Dublin to find, in ironic counterpoint, the parallels with the *Odyssey*. But mining for myth in Narayan may be digging too deep, because everything is there on the surface. Raman in *The Painter of Signs*, though a modern rationalist himself, can casually refer to the legend of King Santhanu; the irony of the comparison, in so far as it is there at all, may be merely local and incidental. In a Hindu culture, where almost everyone is called after a god or a figure from the epics, there may be no special significance in a character being named Savitri. In Narayan it is hard to distinguish between the meaningful use of mythic allusions and the realistic representation of a society in which such allusions are part of people's daily discourse.

All the same, Hindu narratives are central in much of Narayan's fiction, particularly in three novels written in the middle of his career and often identified as the finest of his work, *The Financial Expert* (1952), *The Guide* (1958) and *The Man-Eater of Malgudi* (1961). These are not myths that Narayan uses for the most part, if we think of myths narrowly as narratives about the gods. They are not always even legends, the traditional tales retold by Narayan himself in his *Gods, Demons and Others* (1964), forerunner to his re-working of *The Ramayana* (1972) and *The Mahabharata* (1978). But if we accept a broader definition of myth as any stories that carry a deep meaning within their culture then it may be helpful to identify them as myths. However, such myths are so embedded in the familiar landscape of Malgudi, the recognizable realities of contemporary South Indian culture, that their meanings are hard to interpret. Such attempted interpretation is the subject of this chapter.

The Financial Expert is a fable as much as a myth, the fable of a man who prays for the wrong thing and is ruined by the granting of his prayers. Or rather, Hinduism being a polytheistic religion, it is the case of someone devoting himself entirely to one goddess to the disastrous exclusion of another. Margayya, the 'financial expert' of the title, is a self-appointed, unauthorized loans 'adviser' betraying the uneducated villagers who need money from the bank into a labyrinth of debt. In despair at the loss of his account book on which his business depends, facing the prospect of poverty, he undertakes an extended programme of worship to Lakshmi, Goddess of Wealth. She can give him what he wants, the temple priest assures him: 'When she throws a glance and it falls on someone, he becomes rich, he becomes prosperous, he is treated by the world as an eminent man, his words are treated as something of importance' (*FE* 50, 57). But, as the priest also warns him, such favour will come at the expense of favour from the Goddess Saraswathi who presides over knowledge and enlightenment. 'There is always a rivalry between' Lakshmi and Saraswathi, 'between the patronage of the spouse of Vishnu and the spouse of Brahma' (*FE* 50, 57). And so it falls out. Margayya becomes wealthy as the result of publishing a sex manual, given to him in strange circumstances by the shadowy Dr Pal, and is able to move on to loan-sharking on a grand scale. But his hopes for a brilliant career for his son are constantly frustrated as Balu proves ineducable. In spite of all Margayya's string-pulling influence, his payment of private tutors for Balu, the boy is incapable of progressing in the realm of Saraswathi. Twice, once with the account book and subsequently with the school register that holds his terrible record of marks and attendance, Balu wilfully destroys a key book, emblem of the world of the written. It is the spoiled son, abetted by Dr Pal, who is responsible finally for the collapse of Margayya's fortunes, leaving him at the end more or less where he was when he started.

The fable like quality of the novel is accentuated by the unexplained oddity of the meetings with Dr Pal. Margayya first encounters him by a remote lake where he has gone in search of a red lotus flower required for his devotions to Lakshmi. In response to Margayya's fears that he may be 'a ghost or a maniac', the man introduces himself as 'Dr Pal, journalist, correspondent and author' (*FE* 63, 72), who has retired here to compose his sociological treatise 'Bed-Life or the Science of Marital Happiness' (*FE* 67, 77). Margayya is appalled by the explicitness of the book's treatment of the subject of sex, but at a second, equally accidental meeting with Pal, when Margayya is still desperate for money, he is tempted by the offer of the manuscript. Pal is prepared to give all rights in it to Margayya for the meagre contents of the latter's purse. From the moment of this folk-tale bargain, it is evident that Dr Pal is Mephistopheles to Margayya's Faustus. He is the sinister figure, disappearing and reappearing in the narrative, who sets Margayya up in his grandiose and evidently dishonest loans business, who leads Balu into debauchery and finally blows the whistle on Margayya when his time is up. Pal the tempter and deceiver is never plausibly motivated, coming from outside the normal story space of Malgudi.

With its fable like form, *The Financial Expert* functions as a satire on capitalism. The central character's real name is Krishna, but everyone knows him as Margayya, a soubriquet explained on the first page: '"Marga" meant "The Way" and "Ayya" was an honorific suffix: taken together they denoted someone who showed the way. He showed the way out for those in financial trouble' (FE 1, 1). Instead of a religious pathfinder, who teaches enlightenment, as Krishna himself does to Arjuna in the *Bhagavad-Gita*, Margayya points the illusory way to material liberation.[4] From his first appearance seated under the banyan tree, outside the Central Co-operative Land Mortgage Bank as consultant to the unfortunate peasants come to seek bank loans, through his later more imposing manifestations, Margayya is a 'financial mystic' (FE 124, 140). As such his skills consist in manipulating the mere imagination of money. It is noticeable that in the brief period when his income is derived from a tangible business, the printing of copies of his book *Domestic Harmony* (the wonderfully euphemistic title the printer substitutes for *Bed-Life*), he finds it completely unsatisfying. Though it is making him money, 'it did not seem to Margayya an adult business; there was really no stuff in it; there was not sufficient adventure in it; there was nothing in it' (FE 118, 132). These are pointedly ironic terms of dispraise. The problem with book production for Margayya is that there *is* real 'stuff' in it, ballasting the purer 'nothing' of the money market. He sells out his rights in *Domestic Harmony* to the printer, and sets up in the business he truly loves, leading needy or greedy clients into a maze of loans and mortgages from which in the end only he will benefit. In the final megalomaniac phase of his operations, he tries to corner all the money of Malgudi by running a Ponzi scheme, paying huge interest rates to initial investors out of new investors' capital. Narayan's target of attack, moreover, is not just the 'financial expert' himself but the economic system that accords credit to such expertise. The success of Margayya's Ponzi scheme is facilitated by the black economy of war profiteers who want to salt away their cash beyond the scrutiny of tax accountants. Sixty years on from that Second World War context, the global credit crisis of 2008 once again gave topical currency to Narayan's fable of money and its chimerical obsessions.

This sort of political resonance, however, makes *The Financial Expert* 'more than a social comedy and not just a religious fable'.[5] The question is how to construe the effect of its elusive form. At one level, Margayya can indeed be taken as a conventional cautionary tale: of the five-fold evils of Hindu belief according to one classification, 'lust, anger, miserliness, egoism and envy' (*Ramayana* 8), Margayya displays the effects of all but lust. Yet his weaknesses are psychologized and historicized. His desperate need for money is associated with a subaltern need for the self-respect which he is denied. The threatening figure of the Secretary of the Bank who comes to warn Margayya off the premises is:

> a very tidy young man who looked 'as if he had just come from Europe', Margayya reflected. Looking at him, he felt himself to be such a contrast with his brown *dhoti*, torn shirt, and the absurd little tuft under the black cap. (*FE* 17, 20)

This is the internalized oppression of the colonized. The incident of Margayya's encounter with the ragged men begging money for the burial of an unclaimed corpse takes us deeper still into the sources of his insecurity. Though initially this only provokes the thought that 'money was men's greatest need, like air or food' (*FE* 28, 32), its significance emerges much later in the novel, when it is revealed that 'there was a family secret about his caste which stirred uneasily at the back of his mind' (*FE* 183, 206): some of his ancestors had been corpse bearers. His new riches and status in Malgudi ensure that a marriage can be arranged for his son without any potential father-in-law disposed to look into this stain on his caste pedigree. Margayya's twin needs of unlimited money for himself and escape up and away for his son – 'He could go to America and obtain degrees, and then marry perhaps a judge's daughter' (*FE* 29, 33), he fantasizes – are a flight from humiliation, death and defilement.

The fabular design of the novel's narrative is complicated both by its social specificities, its setting in late colonial Malgudi, and its intermittent interiority. Fables, on the whole, do not need to give their characters a full inner life; a single precipitating moment of realization, like the Prodigal Son as a hired hand feeding swine and determining to go home (*Luke*, 15:18), is enough. For most of the book, Margayya's wife has a purely functional role, as the conventionally silent and submissive partner, only once even named as Meenakshi (*FE* 155, 176). And yet, at a key moment in the face off between father and son, we are taken inside Meenakshi's alienated point of view, watching 'the trouble brewing between them as if it all happened behind a glass screen' (*FE* 138, 156).

> She understood that the best way to attain some peace of mind in life was to maintain silence; ultimately, she found that things resolved themselves in the best manner possible or fizzled out. She found that it was only speech which made existence worse every time. . . . She attained thereby great tranquility in practical every-day life. (*FE* 137–8, 155–6)

This glimpse of the inner life of the wife makes all the more poignant the gap of communication when we move back to Margayya's viewpoint, deeply torn between anger and sympathy for his son, who can only see his wife as 'that stony-faced woman who stood at the doorway of the kitchen and relentlessly watched' (*FE* 138, 157).

A part of the book's power derives from the reader being forced to share the claustrophobic perspective of Margayya's growing obsessiveness, and the consequent numbed inability to feel normally. When the news comes of the death of Balu, who has run away from home, overlaying Margayya's genuine sense of grief are feelings of irritation at the demands that the crisis makes on him and fears that, because of it, he will be forced into reconciliation with his hated brother who is rallying round the family. There follows a dream like episode in which Margayya travels to Madras in search of his son's body, only to discover that Balu is still alive, and that the news of his death came from a madman who sent out the message as part of his 'mission in life to inform at least ten mortals about Death each day' (*FE* 169, 192). This, and the uncannily knowledgeable and helpful police inspector who uncovers the mystery of Balu's supposed death do not seem to be decipherable as part of the cautionary tale of Margayya's misguided pursuit of wealth. They belong to some other order of symbolic imagination through which we travel as bewildered as the bewildered Margayya himself.

In the final part of the book, Margayya's double obsession with his son and his money gathers force. The more feverishly avaricious he becomes, the more indulgent he is to Balu, sparing no expense in arranging for him a marriage, a grand separate establishment, every luxury he denies himself. Inevitably, the love he lavishes on his son brings no reward but the very opposite. Balu, under the tutelage of Dr Pal, grows more and more corrupt and it is when the outraged Margayya discovers the extent of Balu's depravity and Pal's responsibility for it, that the catastrophe is precipitated and his fortunes collapse. The frustrating recalcitrance of the one human being for whom he really cares is a part of the ironic network of cause and effect in which Margayya finds himself trapped. It also makes of the book's ending something much more ambivalent than the moral of the fable we might expect. Dispossessed of their grand house, Balu, his wife and young son, take refuge back with the bankrupt Margayya. As all that remains of his former possessions, Margayya offers his son the pen and ink-bottle with which he ran his original business under the banyan tree: 'I am showing you a way. Will you follow it?' It seems very unlikely that the dullard Balu will have the wit to do so, and it will be Margayya himself that has to go back to his post in front of the bank. In the meantime, he resolves to play with his grandson: 'Life has been too dull without him in this house' (FE 218, 245). As so often in Narayan, we are returned to the situation at the beginning of the novel. But is it a reassuring return to normality, or a satiric indication that Margayya has learned nothing from his experiences, and the cycle is set to start over again? The form of the fable in *The Financial Expert*, intercut with other sorts of narrative perspective, creates a variegated fictional texture to be found again, still more richly achieved, in the two novels that followed it.

GUIDE AND DANCER

The Guide stands at the centre of Narayan's life and work. Written in 1956, on his first visit to the United States, it was published in 1958 as the eighth of his fifteen novels. It won him the award of the Sahitya Akademi, India's National Academy, allowing him to make an impish injoke in *The Man-Eater of Malgudi* where the anti-government journalist accuses the

Sahitya Akademi of 'wasting funds giving an award to every Tom, Dick and Harry' (*MM* 189, 138). It has become his most famous single book, if in part because of the 1965 Hindi film adaptation directed by Vijay Anand, with a US version produced by Tad Danielewski, a film which Narayan himself detested; his essay 'Misguided Guide' is a hilarious account of the making of the movie and its – from his point of view – ludicrous misrepresentations of the original (*Nightmare* 206–17). The novel has been much analysed, particularly for its relation to Hindu mythology and belief.[6] Chitaram Sankaram argues that Raju is recognizable as the type of the 'trickster sage', particularly popular in the traditional religious narratives of Tamil culture.[7] Makarand Panjarape cites as an analogue for the story of Raju a parable of Sri Ramakrishna, in which a thief, on the point of being caught robbing a rich man's orchard, pretends to be a holy man, and is treated as such. He reflects, 'I am not a genuine holy man and still people show such devotion to me. What should I do if I was really a holy man?' and ends up converting.[8] This certainly resembles the situation of Raju, the pretend guru who must face the consequences of his pretence. But, of course, there has been much debate on just how genuine Raju's 'conversion' is at the end of the book, and we only arrive at that point after a long and often satiric account of his career as various sorts of charlatan. Hindu parable in *The Guide* is lodged within a markedly secular setting, a modern world in which traditional myth and religious practice have been abandoned or half forgotten. And the story of Raju is told in a double narrative where it is linked with a second figure almost as ambiguous as himself, Rosie/Nalini the dancer.

Released from prison, at a loss to know what to do, Raju finds himself 'beside an ancient shrine' (*G* 5, 3). It is apparently untenanted, without a priest or worshippers. It is only the presence of Raju there, and the reverential attitude of Velan the villager of Mangala, that revive it as a holy place. Soon we hear of the people of the village refurbishing and decorating its pillared hall, the children coming there for lessons, the adults to hear the pronouncements of their newly-created guru. Raju finds it hard initially to sustain his part because of his lack of adequate knowledge:

He began narrating the story of Devaka, a man of ancient times who begged for alms at the temple gate every day and would not use any of the collections without first putting them at the feet of the god. Half-way through the story he realized that he could not remember either its course or its purport. (*G* 18, 15)

This, however, provides a cue for a switch into the first person narrative in which Raju retells the story of his life from his childhood: Narayan has deftly established the convention by which the present action is told in the third person, the intercut autobiography in the first. 'How could I recollect the story heard from my mother so long ago?' (*G* 19, 15). Thus, the account of a religious revival in a jungle village, remote from the town, is matched by the lifestory of a contemporary citizen of Malgudi who has to reach back to his earliest memories to fit himself for his part as guru.

Raju can just recall the pre-modern life of his childhood: his father with the wayside shop and bullock-cart, his mother with her devout tales from the Hindu scriptures. And then came the railways. The present-day action of *The Guide* is located in the 1950s, the time of its composition, with talk of atom bombs and airplanes even among the villagers, a film crew on hand to cover the last days of Raju's fast for rain. Narayan may be foreshortening chronology to have the railway only coming to Malgudi within the lifespan of Raju; there was already an extensive rail network in India by the beginning of the twentieth century. But the introduction of the railway is made to stand in *The Guide*, as in so many nineteenth-century English novels, for the arrival of modernity. Soon the father's wayside shop is left behind and Raju is installed in the station shop, on his way to becoming Railway Raju, tourist guide to all those who come to visit Malgudi.

Narayan's Malgudi is often thought of as a pre-modern site, the sleepy South Indian town which remains changelessly outside the historical movement of the world outside. The next chapter will deal specifically with this issue of Narayan and modernity. But in *The Guide*, at least, it is a centre of tourism, that most quintessentially modern form of movement. Raju caters for tourist consumers who come from all over India, hungry for the sights that Malgudi has to offer. His skill is to be able to adjust his tours, his guide's patter, to the varying tastes of the visitor:

One thing I learned in my career as a tourist guide was that no two persons were interested in the same thing. Tastes, as in food, differ also in sightseeing. Some people want to be seeing a waterfall, some want a ruin (oh, they grow ecstatic when they see cracked plaster, broken idols, and crumbling bricks), some want a god to worship, some look for a hydro-electric plant, and some want just a nice place, such as the bungalow on top of Mempi with all-glass sides, from where you could see a hundred miles and observe wild game prowling around. (G 62, 53)

Laid out here in eclectic array are the consumable sights, ancient and modern, natural and man-made, sacred and profane. Though pilgrimages sites are among them – the source of the holy river Sarayu is significantly mentioned more than once – these are secular modern pilgrims rather than actual devotees. The ecstasy over 'cracked plaster, broken idols, and crumbling bricks' recalls Larkin's ironic 'ruin-bibber, randy for antique' visiting disused Christian churches.[9] But it also gestures towards the interests of one very specialist visitor, the husband of Rosie, whom Raju derisively calls Marco, after Marco Polo the explorer.

Marco is different because of the seriousness of his engagement with the materials he comes to Malgudi to visit. He has no time for Raju's ignorant tourist spiel but sets himself to study in detail the friezes of the local temple. He is deeply absorbed in the cave paintings he finds near the Mempi hilltop where others come simply to watch the game or carry on their love affairs. The result of his research is an important monograph on *The Cultural History of South India* (G 198, 175). While this sort of academic study is of a very different order from the casual consumption of the snapshotting tourist, it too is part of that modernity in which past history is painstakingly reconstructed in all its pastness. Marco is contemptuous of the idea that there might be any connection between the musical notations he deciphers in the ancient cave paintings and the classical dancing his wife Rosie wants to practice. His work is 'a branch of learning', her art is 'street-acrobatics' (G 147, 130). This disconnection from a living present makes of his research, however rigorous and respectable, a dead thing. The irony is that Rosie's dancing, so far from being street-acrobatics, can be seen to parallel Marco's archaeology in its effort to recover the traditions of the past. Her training not only involves continuous practice but the study of the Sanskrit epics with the help of a guru to interpret them for her. Her skill as a dancer, though, rooted in tradition as it may be, soon makes her a highly marketable commodity. 'You know *Bharat Natvam* is really the greatest art business today' (G 162, 143), Raju assures anyone who will listen. Indeed, this classical dance form of South India, originally performed only by temple dancers or *devadasis* (literally 'women of god') was revived in the twentieth century as a very successful secular entertainment. Raju, as the promoter and impresario of the exotically renamed Nalini, uses a version of the same skills of bluff and banter that made him a successful tour guide. The most satiric part of the novel traces the rise and rise of the career of Nalini, and Raju's ever-increasing parasitic dependence on it. Raju here becomes like Margayya, desperately in need of ever more wealth to bolster his own position. 'My philosophy was that while it [Nalini's career] lasted the maximum money had to be squeezed out. We needed all the money in the world. If I were less prosperous, who would care for me?' (G 195, 173). The unreality of Raju's greedy showmanship and his jealous possessiveness of Nalini as his 'property' are accentuated by her indifference to all this spiralling success; she values nothing more than the garlands she is given at the end of a performance.

We only ever see Rosie through the eyes of Raju and must try to decode her significance as one of the novel's central characters by interpreting the mixed signals of his image of her. At the very beginning of the first person narrative, she is placed as Raju's *femme fatale*: 'My troubles would not have started . . . but for Rosie' (G 9, 7). Her strangeness is accentuated by the strangeness of her unIndian name. She first actually appears as one of the weirder sightseeing visitors, a 'girl who had come all the way from Madras' (G 64, 55) and immediately asked to be taken to watch a king-cobra dance to the music of a flute. And when Rosie, rejected by her husband, comes to live with Raju, she becomes for Raju's mother the 'serpent girl', blamed for the seduction of her son and the destruction of her home. His uncle, who arrives from the ancestral village to try to eject Rosie, is even more blunt: 'Are you of our caste? No. Our class? No. Do we know you? No. Do you belong to this house? No. In that case, why are you here? After all, you are a dancing-girl. We do not admit them in our families' (G 169, 149).

That is at the centre of Rosie's uncertain status, she is a dancing girl, a *devadasi*. She makes no bones of the matter when she first meets Raju:

> I belong to a family traditionally dedicated to the temples as dancers; my mother, grandmother, and before her, her mother. Even as a young girl I danced in our village temple. You know how our caste is viewed? . . . We are viewed as public women. (G 84, 73)

Teresa Hubel, in an illuminating article, has traced the history of the *devadasi* from a position of some power and privilege in earlier periods through a nineteenth-century middle-class campaign of denigration that ended with the outlawing of temple dedication by the Madras legislature in 1947.[10] An orthodox Brahmin family such as Raju's of course regards the dancing girl separated from her husband living with another man as nothing but a whore. And yet she is on her way to becoming Nalini, the most accomplished dancer of her age, idolized by all those who flock to see her perform.

This double reputation is something quite different from the typical glamorous Hollywood star whose rackety private life makes salacious reading in the movie magazines. Narayan makes it clear that Rosie is in no way promiscuous, feels guilty about her liaison with Raju, and has a strong impulse of loyalty to her husband even after he has cast her off. The peculiar attitude towards the dancing girl, sacred in her association with the temple, highly skilled in her art, yet classed with courtesans and prostitutes, reflects the apparently contradictory treatment of sexuality within Hindu culture and religion. By western standards, Hindu sexual mores are very repressive and puritanical, with extramarital love affairs regarded as abnormal and unacceptable. It is noticeable that the sex manual marketed by Margayya in *The Financial Expert* is originally subtitled 'The Science of Marital Happiness', on the assumption that it is only married couples who might avail themselves of its instructions. And yet Hindu temples display some of the most beautiful and most explicitly erotic sculptures of any religious art. Raju makes the association when he returns to Rosie's dance practice, after being interrupted by his uncle from the country: 'Rosie was standing where I had left her with her hip slightly out, her arm akimbo. She was like one of those pillar-carvings in the temple' (G 167, 147).

The apotheosis of the 'serpent girl' comes with the description of the snake dance she performs, presumably having learned from the action of the king cobra she watched on her first day in Malgudi:

> She fanned out her fingers slowly, and the yellow spotlight, playing on her white, upturned palms, gave them the appearance of a cobra hood; she wore a diadem for this act, and it sparkled. Lights changed, she gradually sank to the floor, the music became slower and slower, the refrain urged the snake to dance – the snake that resided on the locks of Shiva himself, on the wrist of his spouse, Parvathi, and in the ever-radiant homes of the gods in Kailas. This was a song that elevated the serpent and brought out its mystic quality; the rhythm was hypnotic. It was her masterpiece. Every inch of her body from toe to head rippled and vibrated to the rhythm of this song which lifted the cobra out of its class of an underground reptile into a creature of grace and divinity and an ornament of the gods. (G 212, 188)

In the misogynist European iconography of the temptation and Fall, the sinuous serpent wound around the tree in the Garden of Eden often has a seductive woman's face. This, rather, is the transformation of eroticism, female and phallic male at once, into the very principle of generative life.

The brilliant architectonics of Narayan's double narrative in *The Guide* brings this climax to Rosie's career as a dancer just before Raju's catastrophe. Once the rhythm of alternating the third person account of Raju's present day life as a guru with his first person retrospect has been established early on, Narayan gives over the long central section of the book, Chapters 7 to 10, to the completion of the autobiography told to the disciple Velan.[11] Raju's arrest, for having forged Rosie's signature to obtain her box of jewellery, comes immediately after the snake dance. The following chapter takes him through his trial, imprisonment and release from jail, the point at which the action of the novel opened. Rosie has soared on up beyond

69

Raju's ken, as even he realizes: 'she would never stop dancing. She would not be able to stop. She would go from strength to strength. ... Neither Marco nor I had any place in her life, which had its own sustaining vitality and which she herself had underestimated all along' (G 222–3, 198). It remains for Raju to work out his own destiny in a comparable way.

After the long immersion in Raju's story, it almost comes as a surprise to readers at the opening of chapter 11 to be reminded that they have been listening to a tale told to Velan over the course of a single night: 'Raju's narration concluded with the crowing of the cock' (G 232, 207). The purpose of Raju's storytelling has been to rescue himself from the appalling situation into which he has blundered through a misunderstanding, committed to a twelve day penitential fast to bring on the much needed rains. He is out to convince Velan that such a fast will only be effective if undertaken by a saint, and he is no saint. The unexpected response from Velan is devastating to him:

> 'I don't know why you tell me all this, Swami. It's very kind of you to address at such length your humble servant'.
> Every respectful word that this man employed pierced Raju like a shaft. 'He will not leave me alone', Raju thought with resignation. 'This man will finish me before I know where I am'. (G 232–3, 207–8)

In the first days of his fast, Raju was able to cheat by eating a few leftovers in the privacy of the temple, but from that point on the public spectacle of which he is the centre will leave him no option but to go through with his role as self-sacrificial saint. The pressure of expectations on him is almost like that on Orwell, to act out the will of the Burmese natives to perform his part as white colonial policeman with a gun in his famous essay 'Shooting an Elephant'.[12]

What is the significance of what happens in the final chapter of the book? Opinion is divided on whether Raju becomes the true saint he has only pretended to be or whether ironic ambiguity surrounds him to the end. John Thieme, for instance, argues that the book's conclusion has been widely misread and it 'leaves the question of Raju's possible promotion to sainthood open' (Thieme 104). Certainly the secular jamboree that gathers around the fasting Raju as he stands each day knee-deep in water reciting mantras shows Narayan at his satiric best. There are the crowds of onlookers with the shops that spring up to cater to their needs 'displaying coloured soda bottles and bunches of bananas and coconut-toffees' (G 239, 213) – all this in a district suffering drought and famine. There is the Tea Propaganda Board that opens its tea-stall, '(People drank too much coffee and too little tea in these parts)', and the Health Department drawing an audience into its health awareness films 'by playing popular hits on the gramophone with loudspeakers mounted on the withering treetops' (G 239, 214). The press coverage and the filming of the fast make Raju's plight a matter of national concern, with urgent government telegrams to the attendant doctors: 'Imperative that Swami should be saved. Persuade best to co-operate. Should not risk life' (G 246, 220). This absurd carnival provides a distanced perspective on the supposed 'great soul', fasting, Gandhi-like, for the good of his people.

More than the literalist questions that so irritated Narayan – 'Can you tell me if Raju the *Guide* dies at the end of the story, and whether it rained, after all?' (*Nightmare* 200) – the issue is whether Raju himself changes within. There is indeed a turnaround of some sort, precipitated initially by looking at Velan, the disciple he has come to resent so bitterly, asleep beside him in the temple:

He was now touched by the sight of this man hunched in his seat. The poor fellow was tremendously excited and straining himself in order to make this penance a success, providing the great man concerned with every comfort – except, of course, food. Why not give the poor devil a chance? Raju said to himself, instead of hankering after food which one could not get anyway. (G 237, 212)

He resolves to banish all thoughts of food and 'this resolution gave him a peculiar strength':

He developed on these lines: 'If by avoiding food I should help the trees bloom, and the grass grow, why not do it thoroughly?' For the first time in his life he was making an earnest effort; for the first time he was learning the thrill of full application, outside money and love; for the first time he was doing a thing in which

71

he was not personally interested. He felt suddenly so enthusiastic that it gave him a new strength to go through with the ordeal. (*G* 237–8, 212)

Even at this point, he is capable of some degree of amused self-irony: 'Lack of food gave him a peculiar floating feeling, which he rather enjoyed, with the thought in the background, "This enjoyment is something Velan cannot take away from me"' (*G* 238, 212).

That is the last we hear from within Raju's consciousness. One of the most moving features of the book's ending is the way the narrative, which has alternated between Raju's often self-pitying, self-justifying confessional autobiography and a free indirect style inside and outside his mind, now pans away to the merely spectatorial. Whether or not Raju dies – and Graham Greene, before even the novel was written, was adamant that it had to conclude with his death (*Dateless Diary* 100) – we experience the mystery of disconnection from interiority that underlines how ultimately unknowable another person is. That narrative strategy supports a fundamental uncertainty about identity consistent with Hindu belief. Some degree of self-liberation, what Tabish Khair calls 'existential awakening', is possible: that much Raju's final reflections make clear.[13] But whether they constitute a 'conversion', as in the Sri Ramakrishna story of the thief turned holy man, is undecidable. The irony of the book's title can work two ways: Raju's role as guru may not be essentially different from his function as tourist guide playing out the part people need from him. But as the suspect 'serpent girl' is transformed in the dance into a transcendent vision of fulfilled eroticism, so the denial of appetite in Raju's ascetic renunciation may turn him into a Hindu saint. We cannot know for certain because, in the maya of illusion, the realized secular world that ends with death is all we ever know.

MYTH WITHOUT A HERO

In *The Man-Eater of Malgudi* there is in fact a myth in the narrower definition of a story of gods and demons, and it is inset rather than embedded in the narrative. Sastri, 'an orthodox-minded Sanskrit semi-scholar' expounds the nature of the *rakshasha*, 'a demoniac creature who possessed enormous strength, strange powers, and genius, but recognized no sort of restraints of man or God' (*MM* 94, 72). He cites a number of examples, beginning with Ravana, Rama's antagonist of the *Ramayana*, and concludes with Bhasmasura

> who acquired a special boon that everything he touched should be scorched, while nothing could ever destroy him. He made humanity suffer. *God Vishnu* was incarnated as a dancer of great beauty, named *Mohini*, with whom the *asura* became infatuated. She promised to yield to him only if he imitated all the gestures and movements of her own dancing. At one point in the dance *Mohini* placed her palms on her head, and the demon followed this gesture in complete forgetfulness and was reduced to ashes that very second, the blighting touch becoming active on his own head. (*MM* 95, 73)

Sastri, sole general staff to the meek printer Nataraj who is the novel's central character, is citing these instances of Hindu demons in relation to Vasu, the unstoppable taxidermist who has taken up residence with Nataraj and is slaughtering and stuffing all the animals around Malgudi. And sure enough, the fate of Bhasmasura does befall Vasu, the strong man with an inevitably fatal blow, who kills himself when he swats a couple of mosquitoes on his forehead. The demon is self-destructive as in the original myth, but there is no god Vishnu to play the hero's role in outwitting him. The literalness with which the Bhasmasura story is re-imagined makes all the more puzzling its relationship to the otherwise ordinary, unheroic milieu of Malgudi, so little apparently suited to the epic struggle of good and evil that such myths enact.

If the recollections of Raju in *The Guide* take us back to some dim pre-modern time before the railways came to Malgudi, *The Man-Eater of Malgudi* is datably set at the time of its composition, 1960–1. Early in the action we hear of Sen, the implacably anti-government journalist debating with 'a Congressman who had gone to prison fourteen times since the day Mahatma Gandhi arrived in India from South Africa' on the subject of 'Nehru's third Five-Year Plan' (*MM* 10, 13). The Congress Party, which had spearheaded India's struggle for independence since the return of Gandhi in 1915 and came to power in 1947, had lost popularity by 1960, when Nehru was about to initiate the third of his Soviet-style five-year economic plans. In the novel, also, there are rumblings of the border conflict between India and China that were to lead to the humiliating Indian-Chinese War of 1962 (*MM* 86, 67). We are discernibly in postcolonial India with its perpetual discontents of inefficiency, maladministration and corruption. Power cuts are part of the daily hazards of business (*MM* 91, 70), and we hear of a 'small mountain of road-metal ... meant for the improvement of Market Road [which] had remained untouched since 1945' (*MM* 208, 151). Nataraj, anxious to cure a sick temple elephant, goes in search of the Malgudi animal hospital, and finds only a 'bare field enclosed by barbed wire'. The staff consists of one doctor, who explains that his salary and the equipment are funded by the 'World Quadruped Relief League, Calif' (*MM* 118, 88) where he has been trained, but the building itself is the responsibility of the Indian government, and it is not clear when, if ever, the hospital will materialize as, having officiated at its formal opening, 'our Deputy Minister has no interest in the project' (*MM* 120, 90). The most shocking example of local corruption and its consequences, because so casually mentioned, is the elementary school on the top of a 'rickety terrace which would come down any day' but which was 'certified to be safe' because owned by the municipal chairman. 'Some day when it fell it was going to imperil the lives of a hundred schoolchildren and six or eight teachers' (*MM* 210, 153). Anyone who thinks that Malgudi is a charming comic comfort zone should read *The Man-Eater of Malgudi* more attentively.

It is true that the action starts, as so many Narayan novels do, with what appears to be a pleasantly static situation. Nataraj, sole possessor of his large family home where he lives with his wife and son, makes enough out of his nearby printing establishment to survive, in spite of the fact that he diverts much of his custom to the adjoining Star Press, to give himself more time to chat in his front room to his constant companions, Sen the journalist, and the poet – he is never given a name – who is composing an epic in honour of Krishna in monosyllabic verse. We are certainly allowed to enjoy this oddball group in its freedom from the ordinary constraints of time and money. But this Malgudi stasis is achieved by a constant negotiation of enmities and the power dynamics of everyday life. We hear of the massive intrafamilial disputes of Nataraj's father's generation that have left Nataraj rattling round what had been the joint family home of five brothers and their families. The adjournment lawyer, so-called because of his skill in protracting lawsuits by repeated adjournments, who appears in *The Guide* also, insists on his clients attending his office above a cotton warehouse, where the sneezing brought on by the cotton fluff, puts them at a constant disadvantage (*MM* 77, 61). Nataraj himself, impractical as he so often seems, has developed sophisticated psychological strategies for deferring the demands of his customers without finally alienating them (*MM* 136–41, 102–4).

Into this delicate equibrium of mini-conflicts crashes Vasu the *rakshasha*. He is more naturalized than the unexplained Dr Pal in *The Financial Expert* in so far as we hear the history of his training first as a strong man, then as a taxidermist. But his demonic status, antithesis of all conventional Hindu pieties, is made clear from the start. Even his first appearance, the head abruptly materializing through the blue curtain that kept Nataraj's printing business separate like a sacred space, recalls the demon figures of temple iconography who often appear thus with disembodied heads: 'a tanned face, large powerful eyes under thick eyebrows, a large forehead and a shock of unkempt hair, like a black halo' (*MM* 12–13, 15). In his killing of animals he violates the principle of *ahimsa*, 'the Hindu ethical idea advocating non-injury or kindness to other creatures' (*WM* 255). Nataraj is particularly appalled at the sight in his own attic (commandeered as a workshop by Vasu) of a stuffed eagle, a *garuda*, the sacred 'messenger of God *Vishnu*'. To Nataraj's protests against his killing the eagle, Vasu replies with breathtaking blasphemy: 'I want to try to make *Vishnu* use his feet now and then' (*MM* 63–4, 50). Like all the demons of Hindu mythology, Vasu sets himself up as an alternative power to the gods themselves. His most outrageous joke is to claim that he, as a taxidermist, is a true preserver, the specific role of the god Vishnu (*MM* 133, 98–9). Vasu is thus the antagonist of Vishnu, Krishna in one of his incarnations, and the climax of the skillfully plotted action comes when the whole town has turned out to celebrate the completion of the poet's epic to the point of Krishna's marriage to Radha. It is during the festival parade of that occasion that Vasu plans to shoot the sacred temple elephant.

So what resistance does Vasu the impious destroyer meet from the Hindu community of Malgudi in general or Nataraj in particular? The answer is very little. As Richard Cronin puts it, 'Narayan is a novelist as well as a fabulist, and as a novelist he subjects the values that inform his fable to a bleak commentary'.[14] His fellow Malgudians make the helpless Nataraj feel responsible for the actions of Vasu: his poaching of big game in the Mempi forests, his killing of a neighbour's dog, the appalling smells that emanate from his stuffing business. When, belatedly, the town authorities do respond to Nataraj's warning about Vasu's threat to the elephant, the deputation that waits on the menacing strong man gains nothing but a dislocated wrist for the police inspector (*MM* 196, 143). Malgudi is full of pious enthusiasm for the festival in honour of Krishna, the speeches, music, dances and processions. But when Nataraj, under the pressure of anxiety for the safety of the elephant, shouts out a deafening prayer for Krishna's protection, disrupting the ceremonies, they assume that he has suffered a brainstorm. Confined to the house, unable to take further action to prevent the coming catastrophe, he remembers another instance of the town's limited tolerance for religious enthusiasm. The boy 'who had strode up and down Kabir Street singing all Tyagaraja's compositions for three days and nights continuously' (*MM* 207, 150–1) to showcase the genius of that nineteenth-century composer of sacred music, had his zeal cooled by a year in Madras mental hospital. As Nataraj reflects with dry irony: 'Our Kabir Street citizens had exacting standards of sanity' (*MM* 207, 151).

All Nataraj does and tries to do to stop Vasu achieves nothing; the *rakshasha* in the end destroys himself without the agency of any human incarnation of the god. Rangi, Vasu's mistress, is a highly unlikely substitute for Mohini, the enchanting female manifestation of Vishnu. The daughter of Padma, 'an exemplary, traditional, dedicated woman of the temple', Rangi herself was regarded as merely a prostitute, 'the worst woman who had ever come back to Malgudi', according to the censorious Sastri (*MM* 107, 81). Unlike Rosie in *The Guide*, she is 'perhaps the most indifferent dancer in India' (*MM* 157, 116). The description of her as 'dark, squat' with 'big round arms and fat legs' (*MM* 108, 81) certainly does not make her seem very enticing, though contact with her, even through a restraining iron grille, is enough to inflame the under utilized erotic imagination of Nataraj. Rangi, who risks her life to communicate Vasu's demonic plans, plays a more honourable part in the action than the more conventionally upright and uptight Malgudians, but in the end it is through no agency of hers that he is destroyed.

Several critics have sought to show that the very failure of Nataraj's efforts to combat Vasu is there to draw out an orthodox Hindu lesson. So Edwin Gerow affirms that 'it is not the "plans" of Nataraj that stop Vasu, for Narayan's point is partly that plans themselves and indeed the entire rationale of directed activity is disruptive, demonic and ultimately futile'.[15] John Thieme makes a similar point: *The Man-Eater of Malgudi* 'endorses his [Nataraj's] inertia by suggesting that active human effort is irrelevant in the struggle against demonic forces and that a preordained order determines the outcome of all events'.[16] However, the novel as a whole hardly supports such a devoutly philosophical moral, if only because of the comic treatment of the central character. There is broad irony in the reflections of the timid Nataraj as he wonders how to tackle the armed Vasu in the climactic confrontation: 'Non-violence would be the safest policy with him. Mahatma Gandhi was right in asking people to carry on their fight with the weapon of non-violence; the chances of getting hurt were much less' (*MM* 213, 155). Nataraj is one of Narayan's typical 'little' men in whose consciousness anxieties are forever growing to fantastic proportions. Whisked off by Vasu in a jeep early in the action, Nataraj has visions of being held to ransom in the forests of Mempi, and wonders how his wife will manage to raise the (entirely dreamed up) sum of fifty thousand rupees in ransom money (*MM* 40–1, 34–5). Vasu is Nataraj's nightmare Other, who must be propitiated all the more because of his very otherness. As Nataraj himself confesses, 'I could never be a successful enemy to anyone. Any enmity worried me night and day'. He goes on to tell of the lengths he went as a boy to try to propitiate a school adversary: 'I made myself abject in order to win a favourable look or word from my enemy and waited for a chance to tell him that I wanted to be friends with him' (MM 92–3, 71). This acutely rendered psychopathology of deference is very unlike the idealism of Gandhian non-violence or the wise Hindu passivity Nataraj's inaction is supposed to sponsor, according to the readings of Gerow and Thieme.

Vasu himself shows nothing but contempt for Nataraj's appeasement policy. He approves instead of the occasional aggressive reaction he provokes: 'That is how I like to see my countrymen. They must show better spirit; they are spineless; no wonder our country has been a prey to every invader who passed this way' (MM 131, 97). This is close to V. S. Naipaul's master thesis about India in general and Narayan in particular in *India: a Wounded Civilisation*. Naipaul maintains that repeated conquest in the subcontinent has bred a Hindu defeatism which only masquerades as a positive principle of non-aggression. Of this Narayan's little men heroes are representative, retreating in the face of disruptive incursions from outside into their own self-enclosed nirvana which allows them to ignore the realities around them. I will be returning to Naipaul's critique in the next chapter. But, although *The Man-Eater of Malgudi* unquestionably demonizes Vasu's policy of relentless aggression, it hardly presents Nataraj as a positively passive alternative. Instead, as Ashok Bery argues, the novel 'does not simply endorse passivity and resignation to divine will; rather, it poses questions about these attitudes and about the conceptions of human actions which underlie them'.[17] Narayan writes comedy in which there is an unspoken understanding that the worst disasters will be averted and a return to some sort of normality guaranteed. But the self-destruction of the *rakshasha* Vasu does not carry with it any very reassuring confidence that all is for the best in the best of all possible worlds. As readers we are allowed to enjoy Nataraj's Malgudi world of compromise and concession, while seeing it for what it is.

CONCLUDING CONTRASTS

As I said in the Introduction, Narayan's distinctive achievement can often be best defined by its difference. Two comparable mid-twentieth century novels from Britain and the United States may be usefully set against *The Guide* and *The Man-Eater of Malgudi*. Graham Greene's *The End of the Affair* (1951) has structural features that resemble those of *The Guide*. The action turns on a love triangle between husband, wife and lover, with the lover as the book's main protagonist and narrator; there is, as in Narayan's novel, a double narrative that converges at the point where the account of the past in one reaches the present of the other. Both books are concerned with the manifestation of the sacred within the secular, showing a very unlikely worldly figure becoming a candidate for sainthood. Saul Bellow's *The Victim* (1947) is a novel resembling *The Man-Eater of Malgudi* in its dramatization of the double. Asa Leventhal's life, like that of Nataraj, is invaded by a threatening *alter ego* who takes up residence with him, infiltrates and contaminates his thoughts and his living space. The protagonists in the two novels are in the end relieved not by their own efforts but by the self-destruction of the double.

The End of the Affair is recounted by Maurice Bendrix, starting some years after his passionate love affair with Sarah has ended abruptly and unaccountably. Still driven by bitter jealousy and the belief that she has left him for another lover, he arranges to spy on her, if only to upset her conventional husband who appears unaware of her infidelities. What he discovers, when he acquires her diary – the second narrative source of the book covering the wartime duration of their affair – is that when Bendrix was apparently killed during an air raid, Sarah, previously an unbeliever, took a vow to God to give up her love for him if his life was spared. In spite of the agonizing effect of this resolution, she continues to maintain it, rejecting Bendrix's pleas to return to him. When she dies shortly after, it is gradually revealed that she has been moving towards Catholic conversion: she was in fact secretly baptized a Catholic, and various miracles are associated with her before and after her death. Bendrix, still anguished at the wilful denial of their love, is left fighting to sustain his hostility to the faith that has taken Sarah from him.

It is likely that Narayan had read *The End of the Affair*, published five years before he began *The Guide*, and it is just possible that the configuration of Greene's novel had an influence on his. But the differences are far more striking than the superficial similarities. Greene was writing from within a secular and sophisticated British milieu – Bendrix is a successful (Greene-like) novelist, the husband Henry is a senior civil servant – in which extramarital sex would have been nothing out of the ordinary. It is implied that Henry is impotent and Sarah has evidently had several affairs before Bendrix. The explicitness of Greene's description of lovemaking is in notable contrast with Narayan's: on the threshold of Rosie's hotel room at the critical moment, Raju says only that he 'stepped in and locked the door on the world' (*G* 89, 77). The whole strategy of Greene's novel is to show characters without any form of religious belief struggling against, with, towards an acceptance of Catholic faith. The implied readers of the book are people like the characters themselves, who need to be convinced through the novel's psychological realism of the transition from cynical worldliness to a life of belief. There is no such self-conscious effort in *The Guide*, no such plotted trajectory towards enlightenment, because in Narayan the sacred and the secular live in undifferentiated juxtaposition. Social and ethical judgements have some genuine force; everyone, Raju himself, his mother, Gaffur the taxi-driver, can see that his illicit love for Rosie will have bad consequences. It does, but it also allows her extraordinary talent as a dancer to blossom and with it a vision of the dance that transcends both disapproval and mere commercial success. Greene's plot strains to show Sarah fulfilling the Catholic conditions for canonization including the attendant miracles produced by relics of her dead body. The idea of sainthood within Hindu culture, where a soul goes through many reincarnations, is much less uniform and prescriptive. Raju's life that has seen him transformed from tourist guide though dance impresario and model convict to village guru may well see him finally turned into the self-sacrificing saint he is taken to be. The question can be left open; Narayan's readers, unlike Greene's, do not have to be persuaded to believe.

It is very unlikely that Narayan, who did not read widely in Western fiction, would have known Bellow's second novel *The*

Victim, and would not have needed it as a precedent for *The Man-Eater of Malgudi*. But here too the parallels are of interest. Leventhal is like Nataraj a representative little man, a lower-middle class Jew with a modest educational background who, with some effort, has found himself a job editing a trade magazine for a publishing firm in New York. The incubus in his life is Allbee, the anti-Semitic drunkard who claims that Leventhal engineered his dismissal from a job that led to the collapse of his career. Though Allbee's accusations may be fuelled by paranoid delusion, Leventhal cannot altogether throw them off and finds himself with Allbee as an increasingly threatening and destructive lodger in his apartment. The climax comes when Allbee tries to gas himself – and Leventhal with him. For Leventhal, as for Nataraj, the whole frightening episode is time out from an otherwise normal life: Leventhal's wife is away from New York during a long hot summer when the action takes place; there is a coda that shows the reunited married couple some years later casually encountering Allbee apparently returned to prosperity.

Bellow's novel is a study in anxiety and guilt; apart from the burden of the intrusive Allbee, Leventhal is oppressed by family responsibilities and an awareness of racist prejudice among his Gentile colleagues at work. Though Leventhal is far more aggressive than Nataraj – he is a big man, physically more than a match for Allbee – the psychological struggle is comparable to that against Vasu, with the advantage always being on the side of the irrational outsider. However, in Bellow it is a psychodrama cast specifically within the multi-ethnic setting of postwar New York. Leventhal is constantly aware of endemic anti-Semitism in Gentile America and so comes to suspect it in his Sicilian sister-in-law, or even in a former non-Jewish benefactor. To some degree he takes to himself the guilt projected on him by anti-Semitic prejudice, and it is this introjection that leaves him vulnerable to the accusations of the WASP Allbee. In the homogeneous Hindu culture of *The Man-Eater of Malgudi*, there is no equivalent of this sort of socially constructed insecurity of identity. Instead, Narayan builds his drama of the double around a conflict between good and evil basic to the Hindu mythology of gods and demons. There is no need to naturalize and rationalize Vasu, as Bellow does with Allbee the anti-Semite. Vasu's eruption into Malgudi needs no more explanation than that offered by the orthodox Sastri expatiating on the nature of the *rakshasha*. It may be no less frightening for that. But it does allow for a comic perspective on the disproportion between the grotesquely superhuman figure of the demon and the ordinary ineptness of the society he invades. The accepted background of Hindu fable and myth, surfacing as they recurrently do in Narayan's novels, makes for a multi-dimensional imaginative space that cannot be reduced either to the extended tropes of self-conscious allegory or to the representational realism of traditional Western fiction.

4

Malgudi and Modernity

In a profile of Narayan, published in the *New Yorker* in 1962, Ved Mehta evokes the writer as a sort of innocent abroad in the big city: the small town, vegetarian South Indian bewildered at the experience of New York. 'Oh, Lard', he exclaims when confronted with a whistling kettle, 'what is this modernity, all these gadgets and such?'[1] (Earlier in the piece, Mehta has explained that Narayan 'spoke a certain sort of Indian English; he made some of his "o"s into "a"s'.)[2] There is a sense, though, that Narayan enjoyed playing up to this image. In *My Dateless Diary*, his account of his first visit to the United States on a Rockefeller Foundation Fellowship in 1956, he portrays himself as helplessly moved across the country from one kindly and protective set of American contacts to another. At this point he was fifty and had never travelled outside India before. But he was to revisit the US many times. Introducing *Malgudi Days*, his collection of short stories, in 1981, he maintained that he could see features of Malgudi in a familiar New York environment: 'West Twenty-third Street, where I have lived for months at a time off and on since 1959, possesses every element of Malgudi, with its landmarks and humanity remaining unchanged' (*Malgudi* 8). Malgudi may be imagined as a small South Indian town, but as a knowable urban community it is not different in essence from a lower Manhattan neighbourhood.

For Narayan is essentially an urban writer. Though his ancestors came from a village originally, he tells Mehta, 'by the time I came into the family, my kinsmen were happily urbanized'. As a consequence, 'neither he nor his characters are villagers ... they are *hommes de ville*'.[3] This reflects

83

Narayan's own life, moving between Madras, which had a population of over half a million even at the time of his birth, Mysore and Coimbatore (where his sister lived), both of them sizable cities. For many years, he wrote a fortnightly column for the Madras-based paper *The Hindu*. The style and point of view in those columns are those of the city dweller, reflecting on the sights and sounds of the streets, the customs of the people he watches as he walks about town. 'Any crowd interests me', he tells his readers, 'I always feel that it is a thing that deserves precedence over any other engagement' (*Writerly* 6). He comments on the lunch-time rush in restaurants: 'Most people are miles away from their homes at tiffin time. This is characteristic of urban life. Students, office-goers, businessmen have no choice in the matter' (*Writerly* 23). He discourses on the experience 'Of Trains and Travellers' (*Writerly* 56–8). His humorous columnist attitude is that of the *flâneur*, musing whimsically on aspects of the city experience that he and his readers share.

The issue of Narayan's engagement with urban modernity is of particular significance because of the way in which it is treated in V.S. Naipaul's influential analysis in *India: a Wounded Civilization*. That book had its origins in a commission by the *New York Review of Books* for Naipaul to go to India to write a series of articles about the 1975 Emergency. Instead of addressing the immediate political issues of the suspension of the Constitution and Indira Gandhi's dictatorial rule that followed, Naipaul set the events of the 1970s in a grand narrative going back to the repeated conquest of India and the Hindu mental condition of defeatist survival which, according to Naipaul, it engendered. An attitude of quietist indifference had enabled Indians to live with the experience of suffering and oppression under the Delhi Sultanate, the Mughals and the British Raj. But it had ill-equipped them to cope with the modern world and the appalling social problems of postcolonial India.

Two novels of Narayan, *Mr Sampath, Printer of Malgudi* (1949) and *The Vendor of Sweets* (1967) are read by Naipaul as emblematic of this developing malaise. The lack of engagement by Srinivas, protagonist of *Mr Sampath*, is seen as characteristic of 'the Hindu equilibrium, surviving the shock of an alien culture, an alien literary form, an alien language'.[4] 'Srinivas's quietism – compounded of *karma*, nonviolence, and a vision of history as an extended religious fable – is in fact a self-cherishing in the midst of a general distress.'[5] This sort of complacent disregard for the modern world and its problems, according to Naipaul, was no longer sustainable by the mid-1960s. So in *The Vendor of Sweets*, a narrative with the same basic outline as *Mr Sampath*, Jagan's withdrawal showing a retreat from an insuperable chaos, has a different sort of significance from that of Srinivas in the earlier book. 'It is as though the Hindu equilibrium required a world as small and as restricting as that of Narayan's early novels, where men could never grow, talked much and did little, and were fundamentally obedient, content to be ruled in all things by others. As soon as that world expands, it shatters.'[6]

Naipaul's is a tendentious argument, and has been indignantly refuted as a reading of Narayan.[7] Still it has had a considerable impact on the interpretation of his work. Naipaul's assertion that 'Narayan's novels are less the purely social comedies that I had once taken them to be than religious books, at times religious fables, and intensely Hindu'[8] is cited approvingly by those who stress the novelist's fundamental Hindu beliefs.[9] Even those critics who regard Naipaul's critique as misapplied, offer a limiting defence of Narayan's non-real comic world, 'a fantastic enclave inhabited by characters who reflect a caricatural reality that can never, no matter how fertile the human imagination, be taken as an approximation to phenomenal reality'.[10] In looking at Narayan's representation of Malgudi modernity as it appears in *Mr Sampath* and *The Vendor of Sweets*, it is worth attending to aspects of the novels that Naipaul ignores: the authorial irony that plays about the characters and situation, and Narayan's degree of alertness to the predicaments of postcolonial India.

AUTHORIAL IRONY

Novelists can put their personal experiences to odd fictional uses. In 1941 Narayan started his own literary quarterly, *Indian Thought*. Largely written by himself and his friends, it lasted just three issues before petering out, though the name was taken over for Narayan's publishing house which, with its steady reprinting of his novels in Indian editions, must have made a great deal of money for him. *Indian Thought* was printed by one M. S. Cheluviengar, well known in Mysore under the name of Sampath. The real-life Sampath was a passionate amateur actor and director who funded his acting habit by running the City Power Press, the 'power' in fact supplied by nothing more than a single treadle. Sampath blossoms into Mr Sampath, printer of Malgudi, the magnetic impresario who not only prints Srinivas's paper *The Banner* but takes over his life, propelling him into film-making when the press is forced to shut down. Narayan was delighted when the original of his fictional character fulfilled his destiny by becoming a 'very busy film personality' (*MD* 180, 157). *The Banner*, a twelve page weekly compounded of local news, crusading attacks on the municipal authorities, and editorial meditations, is very different from Narayan's *Indian Thought*, 'a quarterly publication devoted to literature, philosophy, and culture' (*MD* 171, 149). But the situation of Srinivas, driven by the need to supply copy for his paper, the slave of his printer who is at once erratic and demanding, is a comic version of Narayan's own. The very funny scene in which the timid Srinivas is piloted through the ordeal of appearing before a licensing magistrate by a brazen nut-cracking Sampath was apparently taken directly from life (Ram & Ram 336).

Srinivas is another of Narayan's unworldly drifting protagonists, rather like the moony adolescent Chandran in *The Bachelor of Arts*. But in his case uncertain adolescence has been continued to the age of thirty-seven when he is already married with a child. We are given a retrospect on his prolonged efforts to find a settled occupation: 'He thought of all those years when he had tried to fit in with one thing or another as others did, married like the rest, tried to balance the family budget and build up a bank balance. Agriculture, apprenticeship in a bank, teaching, law – he gave everything a trial once, but with every passing month he felt the excruciating pain of losing time' (*Sam* 11). It is only a blunt enquiry from his long-suffering brother, the lawyer and head of the family who supports him, his wife and son – 'What exactly is it that you wish to do in life? (*Sam* 12) – that drives him to move from his home base of Talapur to Malgudi and set up *The Banner*. His wife and child are sent to live with her parents, and he becomes so absorbed in his editing that he forgets all about them until they turn up in his office one day: repeated letters from his wife and father-in-law have lain ignored in the heap of editorial correspondence.

In this comic picture of the hopelessly impractical Srinivas, Narayan expresses in exaggerated, caricatured form a sense of his own life. In a successful middle-class family, with head-master father and brothers going into professional careers, he was very aware of his own academic failures and the quixotic unlikelihood of his desire to become a writer. The publication of a story in *Punch* gave him credibility enough to convince the father of his beloved Rajam to allow him to marry her, and the appearance of *Swami and Friends* from a London publisher in 1935 was a breakthrough. But his pre-war novels never made him money and he was continually dependent on occasional journalism and family support for survival. After the death of Rajam in 1939, Narayan seems to have been a devoted father to their young daughter Hema. Still he must have been conscious of how much he relied on the joint-family system to take care of her in Mysore on his frequent trips away from home. Narayan was in point of fact a concerned father, a responsible hardworking writer, careful about money to the point of meanness. But in Srinivas there is a sort of guying of his sense of personal and domestic inadequacy, the futility of his *Indian Thought* venture, the disparity between aspiration and achievement.

It is this play of self-irony about the character that colours the experience of the novel and makes of Srinivas something other than the complacently defeated and defeatist figure of Naipaul's reading. So, for example, in a novel set in 1938, the war is looming but *The Banner* remains unconcerned, as its editorial declares: 'The Banner has nothing special to note about any war, past or future. It is only concerned with the war that is always going on – between man's inside and outside. Till the forces are equalized the struggle will always go on' (*Sam* 6). Even Srinivas can see, on reflection, 'a touch of comicality in that bombast' (*Sam* 7). It is as though Narayan is mocking his own disengagement from the great political issues of his time.

He observes in Srinivas the alternating impulses between crusading editorial zeal and indifferent resignation: 'while he thundered against municipal or social shortcomings a voice went on asking: "Life and the world and all this is passing – why bother about anything? The perfect and the imperfect are all the same. Why really bother?"' (*Sam* 30). For Naipaul, it is this latter viewpoint that the novel as a whole endorses, the 'acceptance of *karma*, the Hindu killer, the Hindu calm, which tells us that we pay in this life for what we have done in past lives: so that everything we see is just and balanced'.[11] What he does not see is that this is only one attitude in an ironically represented dialectic that never comes securely to rest in such a position of orthodox acceptance. Whether Srinivas likes it or not, he must struggle with the world as he finds it, an intractable material world of domestic and professional responsibilities, demanding printers and curmudgeonly landlords.

Srinivas's pietistic landlord, in fact, who makes his philosophy of asceticism the cover for his miserly rapacity, is typical. He shows off to Srinivas the amenities of the 'house' on offer, 'a small hall, with two little rooms to serve for kitchen and store':

'You have a glorious view of the temple tower', he said, pointing far off, where the grey spire of Iswara temple rose above the huddling tenements, with its gold crest shining in the sun. (*Sam* 16)

This is contemporary Malgudi. There may be a distant prospect of the temple to Iswara (another name for Shiva) but it is a long way off with a lot of 'huddling tenements' between. Malgudi has a housing crisis because it is a town in the process of rapid growth and modernization. 'Plenty of labour from other districts had been brought in because the district board and the municipality had launched a scheme of road development and tank building, and three or four cotton mills had suddenly sprung into existence. Overnight, as it were, Malgudi passed from a semi-agricultural town to a semi-industrial town' (*Sam* 26). It is this transitional state of emergent modernity that provides the backdrop for most of Narayan's work, a state still familiar in twenty-first century India, in which there is constant movement into the cities from the villages where the vast majority of the population still lives.

The first three chapters of *Mr Sampath* are concerned with the workings of *The Banner* and the backstory of how Srinivas came to set it up with Sampath's help. Then, in chapter 4, the action takes a lurch in quite a different direction, into film-making. William Walsh sees this as a structural flaw – 'the novel's shape is oddly hump-backed' as a result[12] – but it has its own sort of logic. As *The Guide* fast-forwarded readers from an archaic past through the coming of the railways to a time of mass tourism, so *Mr Sampath* jolts us from the nineteenth-century treadle-powered printing press into the age of Bollywood. Once again Narayan was drawing on his own 1940s experience when he, like Srinivas in the book, was recruited as a screenwriter for the commercial film industry. The film magnate T. S. Srinivasan, known as Vasan, an admirer of Narayan's writing, invited him to join the story department of Gemini Studios being set up in Madras in 1941. The cautious Narayan refused this offer but did accept occasional work for Vasan, providing suggestions for some films, full-length scripts for others (Ram & Ram 319–24). For this he received some much needed money (remembered gratefully long after), but he managed to avoid the disastrous effect cinematic involvement had on his American contemporaries F. Scott Fitzgerald and William Faulkner, and he acquired the material for his satiric picture of film-making in *Mr Sampath*.

If Narayan pokes gently indulgent fun at Sampath's rudimentary printing operation, reprised with Nataraj in *The Man-Eater of Malgudi*, his caricature of the movie industry is much sharper. He apparently never had much of an opinion of the business. As early as 1930, he had written a short article entitled 'What is wrong with Indian films?' answering his own question comprehensively: 'Everything' (Ram & Ram 324). It is specifically the ethos of commercial Indian film-making that he sends up in *Mr Sampath*. There is 'De Mello of Hollywood', hired at an extravagant salary as chief executive and constantly deferred to on the strength of his Californian expertise. There is the 'esoteric idiom' of the world of films with every meeting inflated into a 'conference' (*Sam* 93). Above all there is the constant pressure towards the crassest popularization at every level. Srinivas's first offer of a scenario is an exemplary story of a Gandhian hero devoted 'to the abolition of the caste system and other evils of society' (*Sam* 98). All very well but, as Sampath says, 'we need something different for films' (*Sam* 99) something with an opportunity for romance. They settle therefore on 'The Burning of Kama', the mythological story of how the ascetic Shiva, disturbed in his meditations by his attraction to Parvathi, burns up Kama, the god of love, with his third eye. Srinivas's lofty imagination of this subject is repeatedly subverted by the unsuitability of the cast – the veteran lead, a specialist in the part of Shiva, has 'the inconvenient ungodly paddings of middle age' (*Sam* 142) – and the need for a low comic sub-plot. The ultimate travesty comes when it is decided to convert the great climactic scene of Shiva's confrontation with Kama into a dance act. It is at this point that the screenwriter gives up: 'This was one of his favourite scenes. By externalizing emotion, by superimposing feeling in the shape of images, he hoped to express very clearly the substance of this episode: of love and its purification, of austerity and peace. But now they wanted to introduce a dance sequence. Srinivas found himself helpless in this world' (*Sam* 174).

Narayan's protest in *Mr Sampath* is against the sacrifice of the individual artistic imagination to the crudities of the collaborative movie machine. Ironically, the novel itself was to be heavily adapted for a successful Hindi language film, complete with song and dance routines, directed by Vasan for Gemini in 1952.[13] Srinivas in the book, apparently like Narayan, resigns himself to the absurdly grotesque spectacle. He is contrasted in this with another character, Ravi, who ends up as a tragic victim to the film-making process. Ravi, introduced first as an anonymous bank clerk neighbour of Srinivas, always complaining about his tyrannical British boss Edward Shilling, turns (somewhat implausibly) into a gifted artist with an obsession about a young woman whose portrait he has drawn years ago. When Shanti, the actress hired to play Parvathi, turns out to be a look-alike of his lost love, he projects his obsession on to her. Working as a subordinate in the art department of the film studio, Ravi's jealousy is increasingly inflamed by Sampath who has taken possession of Shanti.

When Sampath moves into the screen role of Shiva, after the paunchy actor walks off in a huff, Ravi can stand it no more: he strides on set, grabs Shanti away from Sampath and in the melée that follows more or less destroys the studio, ending up in a state of madness. In an ironic reversal of the mythological script, it is not Shiva that conquers the god of love but love that burns up the whole scene.

The film venture is over, Sampath disappears, and Srinivas is left to pick up the pieces. He extracts Ravi from jail and looks after him in the catatonic state into which he has lapsed. Eventually, he is able to re-start *The Banner* on a sounder financial basis without the assistance of the mercurial Sampath. As he watches Ravi undergo a religious ritual designed to exorcise his madness, Srinivas falls into a reverie in which 'his little home, the hall and all the folk there, Anderson Lane and, in fact, Malgudi itself dimmed and dissolved' (*Sam* 206). He imagines the successive stages of the history of the place: mythical visits to Malgudi by the epic hero Rama, by the Buddha himself, by the great medieval Hindu teacher Shankara, before the coming of 'the Christian missionary with his Bible' (*Sam* 207). He reflects on this mental pageant:

> Dynasties rose and fell. Palaces and mansions appeared and disappeared. The entire country went down under the fire and sword of the invader, and was washed clean when Sarayu overflowed its bounds. But it always had its rebirth and growth. . . . 'What did it amount to?' Srinivas asked himself as the historical picture faded out. 'Who am I to bother about Ravi's madness or sanity? What madness to think I am his keeper?' (*Sam* 207–8)

This passage perfectly suits Naipaul's thesis in *India: a Wounded Civilization*, and he comments accordingly:

> Out of a superficial reading of the past, then, out of the sentimental conviction that India is eternal and forever revives, there comes not a fear of further defeat and destruction, but an indifference to it. India will somehow look after itself; the individual is freed of all responsibility.[14]

But this is to take Srinivas's vision at face value and to ignore the ironic markers that frame it. It is introduced as movie material: 'In that half-dim hall a sweep of history passed in front of his eyes. His scenario-writing habit suddenly asserted itself' (*Sam* 206). And at the beginning of the last chapter we see it turned into grist to the editorializing mill:

> It was late in the evening. Srinivas sat in his office jotting down details of the vision he had had at the exorcist's performance in his house, and attempted to communicate it to his readers. He jotted down the heading 'The Leaf on the Torrent'. He didn't like it. He noted down an alternative title 'The Cosmic Stage: the willy-nilly actor on the Cosmic Stage'. He thought it over. It didn't satisfy either. (*Sam* 211–12)

One of the running gags of the book has been the way Srinivas turns everything into copy for *The Banner*. At the beginning of the book, the totally unexpected arrival of his forgotten wife and child in his office makes him scribble: 'Notes for article for third week. Family life ...' (*Sam* 34). Naipaul solemnly moralizes on rhetoric which Narayan places as the screen-writer's corny dream sequence, the occasion for one more piece of windy pontification.

Mr Sampath follows the pattern of most – though not all – Narayan novels in a return to the *status quo ante*, the normality with which the action opened. But this does not necessarily validate a conservative Hindu quietism, or a reactionary rejection of a wider modernity beyond the Malgudi enclave. In a radio interview in 1968, Narayan summed up the focus of his fiction in significant terms: 'My main concern is with human character – a central character from whose point of view the world is seen and who tries to get over a difficult situation or succumbs to it or fights it in his own setting'.[15] There is no one fixed outcome to this struggle and it does not in itself exemplify a specific ideological or political position. If Srinivas is more inclined to succumb than to fight, that does not mean that Narayan is commending his passivity. His adventures in the media are represented with what one could call sympath-etic irony. There is no doubt a keener edge to the comedy when he gets involved with the films. Narayan's experience with Gemini might have made him share his protagonist's feeling: 'Srinivas found himself helpless in this world' (*Sam* 174). Indian commercial cinema, with its grotesque mixum-gatherum of Hindu myth, spectacle and popular entertainment, was no place for the individual artist. But if Ravi is there to illustrate what happens to those who take it all to heart, Narayan gives the final flourish of the novel to its comic hero, the endlessly buoyant impresario Mr Sampath. When Sampath reappears in Malgudi, having broken up with Shanti, on the run from his movie-making colleagues, he remains his self-confident self, and Srinivas is terrified that he will involve him in further disasters. The book ends with their parting:

> While turning down Anderson Lane he looked back for a second and saw far off the glow of a cigarette end in the square where he had left Sampath; it was like a ruby set in the night. He raised his hand, flourished a final farewell, and set his face home-ward. (*Sam* 219)

Narayan's imagination goes out as much to the free-wheeling and elusive Sampath as to Srinivas on his safe homeward journey.

POSTCOLONIAL PREDICAMENTS

The Vendor of Sweets is not, most people have felt, one of Narayan's strongest novels. Graham Greene, on whose opinion Narayan was always extremely dependent, had reservations about the manuscript when it was sent to him: 'I read your book a few days ago. ... To speak frankly I was a little disappointed with this one. The story line seemed to me to wander a bit and it needs a good deal of editing as far as English is concerned', even though he tried to soften the blow by reaffirming, 'Nothing alters my opinion that you are one of the finest living novelists'.[16] The novel does seem to lose its way at times and there is a sense of Narayan re-cycling previous narrative motifs. Jagan, the title sweet-seller, has an indulged only son Mali, pampered largely because so long hoped for by his previously childless parents, just like Mar-gayya with Balu in *The Financial Expert*. Like so many Narayan figures upset by incursions from outside, the normality of Jagan's routine life is disrupted when a heavily Westernized Mali returns home from some years in America with an American/Korean partner, Grace. It may be that some feeling of the novel's failure led to the unprecedented nine-year gap between it and the much more successful *The Painter of Signs* (1976), a gap Narayan filled with the publication of his version of the *Ramayana* (1972) and his autobiography *My Days* (1973). But *The Vendor of Sweets* has its distinctive differences from earlier Narayan novels in the way it represents its central character and the situation of his time.

Mr Sampath, though published after Independence, is set back in the period before the war. Even if it draws upon Narayan's 1940s experiences in editing and screenwriting, there are no historical indicators beyond Srinivas's one grandiose gesture of *The Banner*'s indifference to world affairs. *The Vendor of Sweets* is clearly a post-Independence novel, dated by a passing reference to the assassination of Kennedy in 1963 (*VS* 56, 42). The colonial era Lawley statue, landmark memorial in so many Narayan novels, is unusually prominent in the book, and we are reminded how much the city has grown since Sir Frederick's time:

> Sir Frederick Lawley faced the city, and his back was supposed to be the back of beyond at one time, the limit of the city's expansion; but this prophecy was confounded when Lawley Extension, South Extension, and the New Extension all stretched out beyond the statue, and Jagan's ancestral home, which had been the last house outskirting the city, became the first one for all the newer colonies. (*VS* 17, 12)[17]

Jagan is a devout Gandhian inspired by the visit of the Mahatma to Malgudi in 1937, presumably the same one where Sriram met Bharati in *Waiting for the Mahatma*. Jagan 'joined the movement for freeing India from foreign rule' (*VS* 41, 31), suffered police beatings and imprisonment for the cause. At fifty-five he still maintains his Gandhian principles, spinning on the *charka* for an hour each day, wearing homespun *khaddar*; at one point, in deference to the teaching of the Master, he even tanned his own leather from the hide of cattle that had died of natural causes (*VS* 9, 6). He has lived on to become a prosperous confectioner, sitting in the midst of his business each day reading the *Bhagavad Gita* in Sanskrit.

For Naipaul, Jagan is symptomatic and the failure of the novel is bound up with the failures of postcolonial India.

The Vendor of Sweets, which is so elegiac and simplistic, exalting purity and old virtue in the figure of Jagan, is a confused book; and its confusion holds much of the Indian confusion today. Jagan – unlike the hero of *Mr Sampath* in pre-Independence India – really has no case. His code does not bear examination.[18]

The Vendor of Sweets may or may not be a confused book, but it is certainly not 'elegiac and simplistic', and Narayan sees as well as Naipaul the inadequacies of Jagan's Gandhianism in the post-Gandhian state. Jagan may be absorbed in his pious reading, but he is constantly alert to the conduct of his business, calling out instructions to the cooks, the shop assistant or the watchman 'without lifting his eyes from the sacred text' (*VS* 12, 8). In Christian terms, Jagan is adept at simultaneously serving God and Mammon. His Gandhian code has room for loopholes. He has a special category of extra cash made from after-hours sales on which he pays no tax: 'If Gandhi had said somewhere, "Pay your sales tax uncomplainingly", he would have followed his advice, but Gandhi had made no reference to the sales tax anywhere (to Jagan's knowledge)' (*VS* 111, 83).

So far from 'exalting purity and old virtue' in Jagan, Narayan points up everywhere the contradictions, self-deceptions and unreality of his principles and practice. The follower of Gandhi, saviour of the poor, the outcast and the destitute, as a well-to-do post-Independence citizen has standard bourgeois views: 'Disgraceful that our nation cannot attack this problem of vagrants. Must do something about it, when I find the time' (*VS* 30, 23). He re-writes the past in self-heroizing fashion:

> 'I had to leave the college when Gandhi ordered us to non-cooperate. I spent the best of my student years in prison', said Jagan, feeling heroic, his reminiscential mood slurring over the fact that he had failed several times in the B.A., ceased to attend the college, and had begun to take his examinations as a private candidate long before the call of Gandhi. (*VS* 27, 20)

Jagan's Gandhianism has committed him to theories of health and diet expounded in a book that sits awaiting publication in Nataraj's Truth Printing Works. Even when his much-loved wife is dying of a brain tumour, he continues to press the merits of nature cures on the infuriated doctor: 'You'll see for yourself, Doctor, when I publish my book. I've all the material for it' (*VS* 37, 27). Few Narayan protagonists are so incisively satirized as Jagan the postcolonial Gandhian.

In Jagan the radical doctrines of Gandhi have fossilized into a sort of know-nothing isolationism. But he is representative also in his simultaneous fear of and awe for Western modernity. He is appalled when he first hears of his would-be writer son's plans to go to America to be taught creative writing. 'Did Valmiki go to America or Germany in order to learn to write his *Ramayana*?' (*VS* 45, 34). America, Jagan is convinced, is a country where Mali will 'corrupt his body with wine, women, and meat, and his soul with other things' (*VS* 47, 35). However, when Mali does indeed go, having stolen the airfare from his father's cash hoard, Jagan is soon boasting about his son in America, buttonholing anyone who can be persuaded to listen about the wonders of 'American landscape, culture, and civilization' (*VS* 55, 41). His postcolonial cringe clashes most obviously with his traditional conservatism when Mali returns to Malgudi with his mixed race 'wife' Grace. It is one thing to have a son gloriously returned from America, quite another to have a casteless daughter-in-law regarded by his relations as a 'beef-eating Christian girl' (*VS* 141, 107). That is bad enough but when Jagan discovers, from Grace herself, that she and Mali are not married at all, not even according to some non-Hindu American ritual, he can only recoil in horror at the couple 'living in sin' who have 'tainted his ancient home' (*VS* 135, 102).

Grace, with her effusive enthusiasm for India and her pathetic efforts to behave like a proper Hindu daughter-in-law chalking auspicious signs on the doorstep, is treated quite sympathetically in the book. It is Mali, the good-for-nothing Indian stupidly mimicking Western ways, who is most thoroughly mocked. The vignette of him emerging from his father's house is telling: 'He wore a fancy dressing gown, and had stuck his feet into slippers. He seemed to cower back and recoil from the bright Indian sunlight' (*VS* 144, 109). The get-rich-quick scheme that Mali has brought back from the US to Malgudi, and tries to bully his father into supporting financially, is an absurd idea of marketing story-writing machines. The machine is designed for the mass manufacture of stories by the manipulation of four knobs for characters, emotions, complexities and climax. 'It is a must for every home', runs Mali's sales talk; 'all a writer will have to do is own one and press the keys, and he will get the formula on a roll of paper, from which he can build up the rest' (*VS* 77, 58). When Jagan starts to chatter on about the oral tradition of the ancient Indian epics, Mali cuts him off abruptly: 'Oh, these are not the days of your ancestors. Today we have to compete with advanced countries not only in economics and industry, but in culture' (*VS* 78, 59).

Narayan is here re-working a satiric concept first used in his essay 'A Writer's Nightmare'. That newspaper column was a send up of Indian bureaucracy, the nightmare an imagined establishment of a government controller of stories, with a Central Story Bureau to license and vet 'plot, character, atmosphere and climax'. Anyone writing without due authorization from this agency 'will be fined five hundred rupees and imprisoned for a period not exceeding eighteen months' (*Nightmare* 70). The attack here – and it is a light-hearted piece – is on the centralized government policies of Nehruvian socialism with its Five-year Plans and top-down control. The story-writing machines in *The Vendor of Sweets* glance instead at American creative writing programmes and the substitution of learned formulaic technique for original creativity. Here, as with the mockery of film-making in *Sampath*, what Narayan feels moved to defend is the individuality of the artistic imagination. In both cases what threatens creative integrity is not Westernizing modernity itself but the derivative Indian responses to it.

Narayan rarely uses imagistic symbolism in his books, but the Lawley statue becomes a suggestive topos through *The Vendor of Sweets*. Itself a memorial to the colonial era, the vagrant who hangs round its base is a reminder of the unresolved problems of poverty in independent India. Jagan's varying attitude towards the homeless beggar is symptomatic, from middle-class outrage – 'Disgraceful that our nation cannot attack this problem of vagrants' – to a more charitable response. It is at the statue, close to his own home, that Jagan frequently stops to take stock and reflect on his situation. And it is there in the book's penultimate chapter, that he spends a night re-living in memory the whole history of his early life, his arranged marriage to a girl from a village, and its consequences. Although this comes so late on in the novel, it works (as so often in Narayan) as a way of giving a quite new dimension to a character who has been largely accepted as a stock figure: the earnest Gandhian with his double standards of principle and practice, the young freedom fighter grown into postcolonial fat cat, the timidly provincial Indian father in awe of his beloved son with his Western ways. Suddenly there is offered a view of how he became the person he now is, an immersion in the circumstances of his early life. As a despised younger brother he had to be coached through the elaborate ceremonies involved in the inspection of the potential bride, the betrothal and wedding. We see how he came to feel for his wife Ambika not only love, but a sexual passion (unusual in Narayan) that obsessed him to the exclusion of normal participation in the joint family, not to mention completing his studies. This aberrant behaviour, from an Indian point of view, lowered his familial credit rating still further, all the more because (in spite of their rapturous love making) Jagan and Ambika were for long unable to have a child. It is only after a pilgrimage to a temple shrine that Ambika becomes pregnant and Mali is born. The completely disproportionate idolatry of the son, made all the more intense after the death of his mother, is given another sort of meaning in the light of this emotional pre-history.

At the base of the Lawley statue, which stands for the historical past in the present, Jagan relives his own transition from bachelor to householder, from the first to the second phase of life according to the orthodox Hindu scheme of things. It prepares him psychologically for the decision he takes in the final chapter to move on again to the last state of *sanyasi*, withdrawing from family connections to a life devoted to piety in the restoration and cultivation of the image of a goddess. This has been prepared for in a strange episode earlier in the novel, where the mysterious hair-dyer, ex-sculptor's apprentice, leads Jagan to where his master the sculptor used to work and retrieves the abandoned image of the goddess from a lotus covered pond. In *The Bachelor of Arts*,

Chandran's time as a would-be *sanyasi* is seen to be inappropriate, freakish behaviour for a young man who should be moving on to marriage and householding, as indeed by the end of the novel he does. For Jagan it is the right time for such a change of life and it represents for him a real liberation of the spirit. His unnamed cousin, the parasite newscarrier and fixer of the book, the spirit of contemporary Malgudi, comes breathlessly to Jagan to reveal that Mali has been arrested for possession of alcohol. He is full of plans to suborn witnesses to blacken the character of the arresting policeman, but Jagan will have none of it. He will bail Mali out of jail, he will pay for a lawyer to defend him but then his son must stand his chances in court: 'A dose of prison life is not a bad thing. It may be just what he needs now' (*VS* 184, 141). He feels a new degree of obligation to Grace, whom Mali has now cast off, having used up all her money. He tells the cousin 'if she ever wants to go back to her country, I will buy her a ticket. It's a duty we owe her. She was a good girl' (*VS* 185, 141). There is a sense of his withdrawal as a means of escaping the entanglements of corrupt Malgudi life but it is not, as Naipaul terms it, 'the ultimate Hindu retreat, because it is a retreat from a world that is known to have broken down at last'.[19] For Jagan, on the contrary, it is some sort of renewal of his Gandhian vows, a return to the first principles of truth and integrity compromised in the postcolonial period. But even more it is placed as the appropriate last stage in an individual life-history, giving Jagan a certainty and a detachment he has never had before.

Throughout his fiction Nararyan registers the stages of modernity in action. So in *The Dark Room* we are told:

> Malgudi in 1935 suddenly came into line with the modern age by building a well-equipped theatre – the Palace Talkies – which simply brushed aside the old corrugated-sheet-roofed Variety Hall, which from time immemorial had entertained the citizens of Malgudi with tattered silent films. (*DR* 22)

Ramani and Savitri are more than happy to sit through the four hours of the Tamil movie about Kuchela, the boyhood friend of Krishna, but already their young son Babu sneers at a mere

'Indian film' contrasted with the wonders of Shirley Temple in *Curly Top* – which was in fact released in 1935. In Narayan's last full-length novel, *The World of Nagaraj* (1990), the protagonist's bullying brother from the village is heavily invested in gobar gas, cutting edge technology for creating sustainable energy from cowdung. Narayan observes modernity but only, as it were, out of the corner of his eye. It is a contingent rather than an essential condition of the fiction he creates. He is unimpressed, unawed by modernity, and does not accept the claims made for it as an all-changing force. For him the human comedy with which he is concerned does not really alter in essence. It may well be that his sense of constantly recurring patterns of human behaviour is underpinned by Hindu belief. But it certainly does not take the form of a resigned acceptance of things as they are, in the caricature of Hindu fatalism attributed to Narayan by Naipaul: quite the opposite, what his characters struggle with is the changing nature of things including the changes that modernity brings.

If *The Vendor of Sweets* seems a weaker novel than *Mr Sampath*, it may be more due to a failure of the comic imagination than Narayan's greater confusion in the face of 1960s India. Mali's story-writing machines are too slight and unbelievable a conception to bear the weight of satire that the plot requires of them, by contrast with the wonderfully grotesque and all too credible extravaganza of the *Burning of Kama* film. (The 'switching-on' ceremony initiating the filming, with the camera garlanded like a god, is one of the farcical highpoints of Narayan's fiction (*Sam* 130–6)). While the daily routine of the confectioner's shop is well realized, by comparison with Narayan's best work there is some thinness to the writing and a jerky quality to the development of the action. What *Mr Sampath* and *The Vendor of Sweets* share is the harassed anxiety experienced by both Srinivas and Jagan in trying to maintain meaning in their lives within the context of a modernizing environment. In the books' satire there is an authorial defence by Narayan of the vulnerable area of individual artistic creativity in the face of the commercialization of modern mass production. But even this is distanced by irony and an awareness of the narcissistic self-protectiveness of the ego involved. Narayan does not set Malgudi as a stably contained Hindu enclave against a wider modern world; he sees it rather as an organic community responding to the powers and pressures of the colonial and then the postcolonial periods. It is within such an urban space that he conceives the existential struggle of his uncertain hero 'who tries to get over a difficult situation or succumbs to it or fights it in his own setting'.

5

Storytelling styles

In the prefatory chapter to *Gods, Demons, and Others*, Narayan writes of 'The World of the Storyteller': 'He is part and parcel of the Indian village community, which is somewhat isolated from the main stream of modern life'. He goes on to imagine this 'grand old man who seldom stirs from his ancestral home on the edge of the village' and the ritual involved in his storytelling:

> When people want a story, at the end of their day's labours in the fields, they silently assemble in front of his home, especially on evenings when the moon shines through the coconut palms.
>
> On such occasions the storyteller will dress himself for the part by smearing sacred ash on his forehead and wrapping himself in a green shawl, while his helpers set up a framed picture of some god on a pedestal in the veranda, decorate it with jasmine garlands, and light incense on it. ... he is completely self-reliant, knowing as he does by heart all the 24,000 stanzas of the *Ramayana*, the 100,000 stanzas of the *Mahabharata*, and the 18,000 stanzas of the *Bhagavata*. (*GDO* 1–3)

Such an august figure, however revered in imagination, could not possibly be a role model for the twentieth-century Indian writer of fiction in English. Narayan was not a villager and knew little Sanskrit besides the *slokas* taught him by his grandmother; he was not an oral storyteller but a literary writer. In fact, when he did come to retell the ancient Hindu legends and myths, first in *Gods, Demons, and Others*, then in his versions of the *Ramayana* and the *Mahabharata*, there was a mismatch between his natural style and the subject matter. The all but colourless prose that works so well in Narayan's own fiction has a way of seeming wooden and pedestrian when he

102

attempts to narrate the actions and thoughts of ancient gods and demons, epic warriors and heroes. The grand and the fantastic are outside his stylistic compass.

Narayan could never be a traditional village storyteller, but in the first phase of his career he became a skilled newspaper short story writer. He had written short fiction from his early twenties, and it was in fact a collection of some dozen of his stories sent to Graham Greene by Kittu Purna in 1934 that initially interested the English writer in Narayan's work (Ram & Ram 145–8). From 1938 on the stories that he published with *The Hindu*, the Madras-based English language daily newspaper, were increasingly important to his professional income, as his novels made him little or nothing. Written to meet deadlines as often as once a fortnight, designed to fill a limited number of column inches, these were conventionally well-made tales: a scene and situation economically established, a narrative developed, a neat or surprising or poignant conclusion. The title story of Narayan's first collection to appear in Britain, *An Astrologer's Day and Other Stories* (1947) – largely selected from three volumes already published with his own company Indian Thought in Mysore – may be considered typical. We are introduced to the astrologer who has run away from his far-off village and set up shop on the sidewalk in Malgudi, conning his customers with plausible sounding predictions, somewhat in the style of Raju in *The Guide* in his guru phase. A tougher than usual client appears one evening challenging the astrologer to tell him something convincing. Amazingly, the astrologer not only knows the details of this man's past village life and how he survived an attempted murder, but even his name. Convinced by this authoritative display, the customer accepts the astrologer's advice to give up his quest for the would-be murderer (who he is assured is already dead) and return home. In a final casual conversation between the astrologer and his wife, the truth is revealed: 'Do you know a great load is gone from me today? I thought I had the blood of a man on my hands all these years?' (*Malgudi* 19). With that satisfying narrative click, the reader can move on to another part of the newspaper.

When Greene first read Narayan's stories he thought they must have been influenced by Chekhov. In fact, Narayan had not read Chekhov at the time and was never to work in the mode of the modernist short story, image-based and elliptical, pioneered by the Russian master and developed by Joyce, Lawrence and Mansfield. The bulk of his stories, many of them written for *The Hindu*, are like 'An Astrologer's Day', deft, formulaic, and old-fashioned in their narrative form. The best of his later short fiction is looser, like the situational 'A Horse and Two Goats', the disturbingly psychological 'A Breath of Lucifer', or the anecdotal reminiscence of Narayan's own gardener 'Annamalai'.[1] Narayan could write atmospheric and imaginative stories, but the shorter they were the more he tended to fall back on sentimental or moralistic narrative shapes. He needed the greater amplitude of at least the novella, if not the novel, to achieve the complexity of texture and subtlety of effect that were his real strengths. Throughout his work, however, we are always conscious of the story-telling momentum of the fiction and the presence of more or less reliable story-tellers within the stories. His later books in particular illustrate his characteristic use of narrators and narration, the interplay between the speaker and the composed story in his chosen style.

NARRATORS AND NARRATIONS

Nagaraj, the hero of *The World of Nagaraj*, has an impossible mission in life, to write a book about Sage Narada. Narada was:

> the celestial sage who had a curse on his back that unless he spread a gossip a day his head would burst. The sage floated along with ease from one world to another among the fourteen worlds above and below this earth, carrying news and gossip, often causing clashes between gods and demons, demons and demons, and gods and gods, and between creatures of the earth. (*Nagaraj* 3)

Nagaraj wants to write an authoritative work on the subject but is handicapped by the lack of authoritative sources. About Narada, the compulsive talker, little or nothing has been written down. Bari, the stationer from North India, claims to have an old volume in Sanskrit containing an authentic account of the sage. But after several sessions of taking down notes from Bari's improvised translation of the text into broken

English and Tamil, Nagaraj has still not arrived at the birth of Narada. At the end of the book, he abandons his task, consigning all his notebooks 'to the old room, where at least white ants may relish my notes on Narada' (*Nagaraj* 185). Narayan's final novel, in the series created out of Malgudi talkers and talk, is about the impossibility of making a definitive written record of the spoken.

Talkative Man also compares himself to Narada at the opening of the novel that bears his name:

> They call me Talkative Man. Some affectionately shorten it to TM: I have earned this title, I suppose, because I cannot contain myself. My impulse to share an experience with others is irresistible, even if they sneer at my back. I don't care. I'd choke if I didn't talk, perhaps like Sage Narada of our epics . . . (*TM* 1)

The irony of the grandiose comparison is evident. TM is a small town would-be journalist, a 'Universal Correspondent since I had no authority to represent any publication' (*TM* 3). He is welcome in all the worlds of Malgudi perhaps, but has difficulty in spreading his stories to the press beyond that mini-cosmos. His big breakthrough comes with the arrival of Dr Rann, futurologist and mystery man, allegedly from Timbuctoo. TM's published piece about 'Timbuctoo Man', accompanied by a surreptitiously taken photograph, brings to Malgudi the first of what turns out to be a whole string of abandoned wives of Dr Rann. The arrival of this woman, the formidable six foot tall Commander Sarasa of the Home Guard Women's Auxiliary force, certainly threatens conflict. But TM is at pains to keep Rann and his pursuer apart. Even when Rann is about to repeat his habitual philandering practice and elope with the innocent Girija, teenage granddaughter of TM's friend the librarian, his impulse is not to cause trouble: 'I had to avoid upsetting anyone on any side' (*TM* 97). TM, with his local stories and his snippets of gossip, his anxiously peaceable intentions amounting to moral cowardice, is a mock-heroic version of the sage Narada.

Talkative Man, Narayan's fourteenth novel, was published in 1986, the year the author turned 80. But the character had been conceived for one of Narayan's first stories, 'A Night of Cyclone', written when he was a student in 1929 (Ram & Ram

88).[2] He was then reused repeatedly as frame storyteller in many subsequent short stories, rather like P. G. Wodehouse's Mr Mulliner.[3] As Mulliner always has a tale to tell his listeners at the bar of the Angler's Rest, so TM holds forth to an equivalent audience in Malgudi's Boardless café. While Mulliner's stories feature the adventures of an apparently inexhaustible set of nephews and cousins, TM is generally his own protagonist. No attempt is made to reconcile the different careers he has had, or to produce a coherent chronology for them. He is an apprentice musician in 'The Snake-Song', a journalist in 'Lawley Road', an archaeologist's assistant in 'The Roman Image', a shopkeeper in 'A Career', agent for a fertilizer company in 'The Tiger's Claw'.[4] The status of these stories is unclear. It seems unlikely that TM can have had so many past lives, proliferating like the family members of Mr Mulliner as further starting points for more stories. The ending of 'The Tiger's Claw', in particular, prompts speculation that TM's narration may have been pure fantasy. The body of a man-eating tiger, paraded through the village by the local hunters who have at last killed him, starts TM off on the bizarre account of how he once found himself barricaded in an isolated railway station defending himself against a tiger by cutting off three of its claws. Sure enough three toes are missing from the right forepaw of the dead beast. But the hunters have another explanation: 'It's said that some forest tribes, if they catch a tiger cub, cut off its claws for some talisman and let it go. They do not usually kill cubs' (*Malgudi* 56).

Stories feed our appetite for vicarious engagement with the strange and wonderful, for gossip and anecdote about the lives of others: storytellers like TM, whether reliable or not, minister to that primary need for narrative. Yet there remains an anxiety about the truth content of the tales told. This is most evident in 'The Grandmother's Tale' (1993), the title novella of Narayan's last published book. For this Narayan returned to his earliest memories of his own grandmother already described in his autobiography *My Days*, and the opening is explicitly autobiographical: 'I was brought up by my grandmother in Madras from my third year while my mother lived in Bangalore with a fourth child on hand after me. My grandmother took me away to Madras in order to give relief to an over-burdened daughter' (*GT* 1, 3). There is further scene-setting taken from his own early life before he embarks on the story his grandmother told him when he was starting his career as a novelist about her own mother's quest for her husband, the writer's great-grandfather. It is a story which Narayan had already used in *The Painter of Signs* as the often repeated moral tale told by Raman's devoutly conservative aunt, illustrating the triumph of the abandoned child bride who tracks her spouse the whole way to Poona in the north, manoeuvres him into returning to the south, forces him to relinquish his second 'wife' by the threat of suicide, and settles down to a successful and prosperous married life (*PS* 36, 31–2). What Narayan dramatizes in 'The Grandmother's Tale', however, is the oral telling of the story, and the efforts of the young writer to give it shape and sense.

The story comes down to Narayan told by his grandmother Ammani, as she heard it from her mother 'when she, Ammani, was about ten years old'.

> Day after day, I sat up with her listening to her account, and at night developed it as a cogent narrative. As far as possible, I have tried to retain the flavour of her speech, though the manner of her narrative could not be reproduced as it proceeded in several directions back and forth and got mixed up with asides and irrelevancies. I have managed to keep her own words here and there, but this is mainly a story-writer's version of a hearsay biography of a great-grandmother. (*GT* 8, 7–8)

Though for much of the tale the frame situation is faded out and the narrative given direct, we are repeatedly reminded of the conflict of viewpoint between the 'story-writer', as Narayan calls himself, and the storytelling grandmother. Narayan wants to pin down details: what village in South India did his great-grandparents come from, what god was worshipped there? Ammani cannot satisfy this sort of curiosity: 'Don't interrupt me with questions, as I have also only heard about these events' (*GT* 9, 9). When the questing wife Bala eventually finds the runaway Viswanath in Poona, long established as a gem merchant, having married the merchant's daughter Surma, Narayan is concerned by the improbabilities of the situation:

I asked the next question, which bothered me as a story-writer: 'Did Surma Bai have no children?'

'I don't care if she had or had not or where they were, how is it our concern?'

'But you say they were living together for fifteen years!'

'What a question! How can I answer it? You must ask them. Anyway it is none of our business . . .' (*GT* 50, 35–6)

The enterprising young woman who goes in search of her lost husband (often in disguise) is a recurrent tale type, used by Shakespeare, for instance, in *All's Well that Ends Well* and again in *Cymbeline*.[5] Such folk-stories do not need the sort of detailed locatedness and verisimilitude that the modern 'story-writer' demands for his sort of fiction. Ethical issues may also be regarded as irrelevant. Ammani builds up a sympathetic portrait of the second wife Surma, her devotion to Viswanath and warm friendship for Bala. Narayan is consequently taken aback when Bala, having tricked Surma into coming with them on a supposed pilgrimage to Bangalore, says that she will drown herself if Viswanath does not send Surma back to Poona and stay with her, his true wife. '"Ammani", I (this writer) said, "I can't find any excuse for the way your mother manoeuvred to get rid of the other woman" . . . "Don't talk ill of your ancestors"', Ammani snaps back (*GT* 65, 45–6). When 'this writer' tries to suggest other more honourable ways that Bala might have behaved towards Surma, the grandmother insists that the facts are the facts: '"You cannot manipulate people in real life as you do in a story", she said' (*GT* 67, 47).

There are complicated ironies at work here. Narayan may be mocking critics of his own who asked the sort of literal-minded questions about Malgudi that he puts to his grandmother in the novella.[6] But he also exposes the way in which the idea of reality plays in and out of the telling of stories. The orally transmitted tale of the wife re-finding her husband, whether literally true or not, is satisfying within a patriarchal culture for its apparent challenge to gender stereotypes coming to rest in ideological conformism. Having re-gained Viswanath, 'Bala turned out to be a model wife in the orthodox sense, all trace of her adventurous spirit or independence completely suppressed' (*GT* 75–6, 53). A greater degree of realistic plausibility may be required for the literary fiction created by a modern novelist such as Narayan, as well as a higher standard of moral and political sensitivity. Yet listening to the oral tale of the grandmother connects the writer to the actuality of lives that gave birth to his own. Narayan's mother could just recall being carried in the arms of her mother Ammani at the funeral of Viswanath, the husband returned from Poona so long ago (GT 94, 66). While the metafictional scaffolding of 'The Grandmother's Tale' makes us continually aware of its constructedness as story, it reaches back through memory to the unverifiable imagination of truth.

IMPERSONATIONS

For the most part, Narayan avoided using first person narratives in his fiction. The English Teacher is an obvious exception, where the novel's closeness to his own experience made it almost essential. In The Guide Raju's story of his past life told to Velan in the first person is set off against the third person account of the present action. Otherwise, The Man-Eater of Malgudi is the only novel of Narayan's narrated by its central figure, perhaps to accentuate the sense of menace coming at Nataraj from the fearsome and inscrutable Vasu. For the most part, Narayan preferred the free indirect style which allowed him to involve his readers in the thoughts and feelings of the main characters, their frequently fluctuating moods, while keeping the distance necessary for comic irony. Introducing Talkative Man, so long a persona of the short stories, into his own novel allowed for a new dimension to the first person narrative. For within TM's main tale of Dr Rann, used to illustrate his storytelling capacity, he himself is forced into the role of listener to Commander Sarasa's obsessive telling of the story of her courtship and marriage by Rann. 'The lady's volubility overwhelmed me. I felt like the wedding guest whom the Ancient Mariner held in a spell of narrative, preventing his entry into the reception whence the noise of festivities was coming' (TM 66). The comedy here is that of the biter bitten, the compulsive talker turned into unwilling audience. Rann is distanced still further until he becomes merely a constructed collage of different versions of himself.[7]

In his later work Narayan clearly became more interested in the effect of narrators and narration. But there is no real precedent for *A Tiger of Malgudi* where a substantial part of the story is told by the tiger. In his introduction to the novel, Narayan says that the idea came to him from the appearance at the Kumbh Mela festival in Allahabad of a hermit with a tiger walking freely among the crowds, and his decision to write was confirmed by what was subsequently identified as a Garfield cartoon, in which Garfield the tiger-coloured cat is captioned saying 'I'd love to get into a good book' (*Tiger* 7).[8] But another prompt for the novel must have been the filming of *The Guide*. In his essay 'Misguided "Guide"', Narayan describes how his director insisted on inserting into the film a scene in which the rivalry between Raju and Marco for the love of Rosie was to be symbolized by two tigers fighting to the death over a spotted deer. Amenable tigers, however, proved hard to find. One 'belonged to a circus and the circus owner would under no circumstance consent to have the tiger injured or killed': the director had been insisting that one tiger had to die in the fight. Another 'full-grown Bengal tiger' was at last found 'occasionally lent for jungle pictures, after sewing its lips and pulling out its claws' (*Nightmare* 213). These details are used in *Tiger* in which the Captain, the circus proprietor who owns Raja the tiger, stipulates in his contract with the film producer that the animal should not be injured, and is disgusted at the thought that it should be mutilated by the sewing of its lips or the drawing of its claws (*Tiger* 100–1, 87–8). Narayan had already sent up the absurdities of the film business in *Sampath* but his experience of the grotesque farce of this episode in the making of *The Guide* – the tiger shrank away from fighting with the leopard hired as a second tiger substitute, and the deer in the end had to be forcibly fed to the leopard (*Nightmare* 213–4) – sharpened the edge of his satire in this part of *Tiger*.

For almost all his fiction writing career, Narayan restricted himself to the viewpoint of a very specific class of person: Tamil Brahmin males between puberty and late middle age. These men may occasionally toy with the idea of becoming *sanyasis*, as Chandran does prematurely in *The Bachelor of Arts* and as Jagan may actually do at the end of *The Vendor of Sweets*, but the regular milieu of the action is the secular social life of Malgudi as viewed by those more or less actively involved with it. For *Tiger*, as a very special experiment, Narayan went outside his normal restricted range, on the one hand by giving his readers a non-human narrator, the tiger, antithesis of the timid, nervously reflective little man protagonists of the other novels, and, on the other hand, portraying an actual *sadhu*, someone who has successfully renounced the secular life of worldly attachment. It was a doubly disengaged way of rendering the normal spectacle of Malgudi.

Hinduism teaches reverence for all forms of life and, in the doctrine of reincarnation, denies that the human soul is inherently different from that in other sorts of living being. Narayan in *Tiger* uses this as his imaginative starting-point for the tiger's eye narrative. Raja tells his story as a confessional narrative from the old age retirement refuge of a zoo cage. He has been taught by his Master (equivalent to the Kumbh Mela hermit) to see his present form as merely one in a sequence of lives. In his efforts at self-transcendence he feels guilty about his predatory animality. At the same time his naturalness as an animal is contrasted with the foolishness, the perversity and petty vanities of the human world. In particular he offers a perspective on the human phenomenon of power and performance.

Narayan had little interest in formal politics but throughout his work he is concerned with the dynamics of power: what gives one person prestige and ascendancy over others within the home or within the community. In Raja's opening account of his early life we are shown the hierarchy of the forest in which the tiger is top cat: 'Every creature in the jungle trembled when it sensed my approach. "Let them tremble and understand who is the Master, Lord of this world", I thought with pride' (*Tiger* 13, 13). There were exceptional creatures who challenged this supremacy, however, the formidably defended porcupine, monkeys and birds mockingly beyond reach, the defiant leopard. As in so many beast fables, the animal community parallels the human, where there are always individuals and groups who stand outside a given power structure. But the casually destructive impact of man upon the animals is demonstrated when Raja's mate and their four cubs are killed and carried off in a jeep. In revenge the tiger becomes a predator on the villages carrying off domestic cattle and sheep. And from this point on, the novel's point of view shifts between Raja's narrative and that of his human antagonists and captors.

In *The Guide* Narayan constructs a careful plot structure to support his double narrative: Raju tells his lifestory to Velan in order to convince the credulous disciple that he is not the saint he is taken to be, and therefore need not continue with his fast. There is no such narrative scaffolding in *Tiger*. Raja's first person story fades out and an omniscient narrator fills in the background of the villagers' reactions to his attacks; we are given the history of the Captain, his early life, how he came to own the Grand Malgudi Circus and be prepared to capture the tiger. At times Narayan hardly bothers to distinguish between what Raja can be imagined to have known (helped by his gradually acquired power of understanding human speech) and what is necessarily beyond him. To enjoy the novel, we are asked to suspend finicky worries about probabilities and simply follow the story as it unfolds. What it sets up by means of the double narrative is a system of parallels, analogues and contrasts between animal behaviour and human performance.

Captured by the Captain, starved and tamed into sub-mission, Raja is taught to perform in the circus ring, to do things that seem to him unnatural, nonsensical. He is made to jump over obstacles, run through hoops of fire, and (most humiliatingly of all) to sip from a saucer of milk in company with a goat. We are made aware of the psychological domi-nance of the Captain with his whip and chair torturing Raja into carrying through this absurd routine. There is even a degree of satisfaction when Raja, goaded too far in one performance, snaps the head off the goat, an anticipation of the novel's climax when the tiger, driven mad by the even more extreme demands made of him during the film shoots, similarly decapitates the Captain. Looking at the dead body of his long-term trainer, Raja reflects coolly: 'It was surprising that such a flimsy creature, no better than a membrane stretched over some thin framework, with so little stuff inside, should have held me in fear so long' (*Tiger* 114–5, 100). The claim of man to dominate the animal world stands revealed as a gigantic bluff.

The Captain is by no means regarded as the villain of the story, however. Within limits, according to his lights, he treats his animals well. Some of them even regard him as their unwitting servant in the circus situation. The ape, communicating in an imagined animal language, comments to Raja, 'we are at least spared the trouble of seeking food and preserving ourselves from enemies. He is doing all that for us. He is a damned fool, but doesn't know it; thinks that he is the Lord of the Universe' (*Tiger* 51, 45). Raja too had thought himself Lord of the Universe: Man's sense of power may be as much an illusion as the animal's. What is distinctive about human behaviour is the performance of parts and roles. Raja meets a puzzling example of this in the constantly quarrelling relationship between the Captain and his wife the trapeze artiste Rita. They are always at odds about the management of the circus and the relative importance of their acts. Rita is particularly outraged by the Captain's plan to have the trapeze girls somersault through a ring of fire: 'I am not prepared to spare any of my girls or set fire to myself just to please your fancy. I'm not an orthodox wife preparing for *sati*' (*Tiger* 58, 51). Yet when the Captain dies, Rita does indeed kill herself in a last jump from the trapeze. Questioned by Raja about the peculiarity of this relationship between the Captain and Rita, the Master tells him, 'You must not forget that everyone is acting a part all the time, knowingly or unknowingly' (*Tiger* 69, 60).

The unselfconscious animal viewpoint of Raja is used to expose the vagaries of human performativity, of which the circus acts and the film scenario are only the most absurd examples. When the tiger, having killed the Captain, wanders at large through Malgudi, finally holing up in the headmaster's study of the school, the chaos produced is turned into a spectacle watched with panic and delight by the townspeople (*Tiger* 115–50,100–30). Raja, having fed full, sleeps soundly; while the schoolchildren have taken refuge in the hall, plans have to be devised to rescue the headmaster who is stuck in an attic above the tiger. Alphonse, the poacher/marksman, dealer in tiger skins, is summoned and succeeds in bribing the representatives of the Tiger Project, the official government preservation agency, to certify Raja as a man-eater allowing him to be killed. (Narayan has obviously very little confidence in Indian state environmental policy.) It is only when Alphonse, getting up the courage to shoot the tiger, drinks himself into a stupor, that the Master takes charge, the Master who refuses to allow the words 'beast' or 'brute' to be used – 'They're ugly words coined by man in his arrogance' (*Tiger* 118, 103) – and who, unarmed, by sheer force of personality, leads Raja peacably out of the school.

The Master shows up first as an unknown *sadhu* at the edge of the crowd. When they ask, 'Who are you?' he replies sententiously: 'You are asking a profound question! I've no idea who I am! All my life I have been trying to find the answer' (*Tiger*, 118, 103). Later on, we do in fact discover something of the former life of the Master, a Gandhian freedom fighter in his youth, a settled family man in Malgudi with a job in an insurance company who left his wife and children to become an unattached *sanyasi* (*Tiger* 152–3, 132–3); towards the end of the book there is a confrontation with the abandoned wife who tracks him down in the Mempi forest retreat where he has settled with Raja. He rejects his wife's appeals to return to her: 'I have erased from my mind my name and identity and all that it implies' (*Tiger* 171, 148). If the story of Raja is there to illustrate the idea that animals as much as humans may have souls and selves, the Master teaches the delusive nature of human selfhood. The split storytelling of the novel is designed to set up a relativist perspective leading readers on to the Master's view of things. From the beginning of Raja's narrative, there is an ironic disjunction between his use of the term 'Master' to refer to his teacher and guru, and his own imagined position in the jungle as 'Master, Lord of this world' (*Tiger* 13, 13). The tiger's mastery of the other animals achieved by superior strength, the Captain's mastery of the tiger based on mental ascendancy, are equally ignorant delusions of the ego. The only true knowledge comes from the relinquishing of all such claims to mastery and the self-belief on which they are based.

The weakness of the novel, however, is exactly the tendentiousness of this sort of statement offered as the moral of the story. *Tiger* is enjoyable as a Utopian fable; it is skilful in its easy alternation between Raja's ingenuous first person narrative and the sardonically broader view of the omniscient narrator. But it forces us to accept the superior wisdom of the

Master, whose pious self-abnegation has a way of seeming merely self-satisfied.[9] Narayan's impersonation of Raja has its charm as the evidently human and anthropomorphic imagination of the animal mind. His characterization of the Master fails because such perfected selflessness is beyond the range of realization for readers, all of whom necessarily live within the imperfection of the self. A belief in the role-playing instability of human identity is fundamental to Narayan; the lives of the people of Malgudi with their volatile social interactions, their fantasies of other selves, constitute a rich embroidery of that belief. The imaginative experiment in *Tiger*, to try to tell the story from outside that ordinarily human self-bound perspective, in the end defeats itself.

THE CHOICE OF STYLE

In *Tiger* we have to accept the hypothesis that Raja has learned to understand human language, can make out what people are saying around him, and can articulate his own autobiography. It is one version of the fantasy of King Solomon's ring, the capacity for humans to speak with animals. But there is of course a much more widespread ventriloquism in Narayan's fiction, his attribution of his own fluent and flexible English to his Tamil-speaking Malgudians. For it would presumably have been in Tamil not in English that Talkative Man told his tall tales at the Boardless café; it would certainly have been in Tamil that Narayan's grandmother Ammani related the story of her mother's husband pursuing pilgrimage to Poona. In *The Vendor of Sweets*, when Mali first declares his intention of becoming a writer, Jagan ponders on the issue of the medium to be used: 'He wanted to know which language his [son's] Muses accepted, whether Tamil or English. If he wrote in Tamil he would be recognized at home; if in English, he would be known in other countries too' (*VS* 42, 31). Narayan himself never seemed to have worried about this choice; he always wrote in English and ignored any suggestions that he might write in his own first language instead.[10]

What is more, Narayan made no effort to cultivate a specifically Indian form of English suitable to Indian traditions of storytelling as recommended by Raja Rao in his much-quoted Foreword to *Kanthapura*:

> One has to convey in a language that is not one's own, the spirit that is one's own. . . . We cannot write like the English. We should not. We cannot write only as Indians. We have grown to look at the large world as part of us. Our method of expression therefore has to be a dialect which will some day prove to be as distinctive and colourful as the Irish or the American.[11]

In this spirit Rao sought self-consciously to write a Kannada-influenced English that could give an effect of the illiterate old grandmother who is the oral storyteller of *Kanthapura*. By contrast, Narayan writes a neutrally correct standard English – the more correct no doubt for the tactful editing of Graham Greene.[12] He does not stud his texts with words taken over from Indian languages as many of his fellow Indian writers do from Mulk Raj Anand on.[13] Such common Indian words as he does use are almost always explained by the context or, in some editions, given in a brief glossary at the end.[14] Narayan does not 'write back' to the metropolitan imperial centre by using a defiantly creolized version of the language. He was in fact impatient with self-conscious literariness of any kind, heretically dismissing the great stylists of modernism; Gertrude Stein and Ernest Hemingway, he was convinced they could 'have nothing to say to me', Joyce and Faulkner were 'bores'.[15]

In the era of Salman Rushdie's 'chutnified' English with its rich, virtuoso display of Indian linguistic hybridity, Narayan's plain style has come in for attack. Shashi Tharoor, cultural commentator, accomplished novelist and evident admirer of Rushdie, compares Narayan's prose 'at its worst' to the 'bullock-cart: a vehicle that can move only in one gear, is unable to turn, accelerate or reverse, and remains yoked to traditional creatures who have long since been overtaken but know no better'.[16] A more representative attitude is an admiration for Narayan's style together with a sort of puzzlement as to how it is achieved. V. Y. Kantak, one of Narayan's most illuminating interpreters, sums up the feeling:

> His very simplicity, his naiveté seems to set a problem. There is so little to expatiate intellectually, analyse, expound, fathom the

116

depth of. And yet the naiveté of Narayan has a quality that haunts us as only art can, when it stands on its own without any peripheral attractions or distortions. Meagre means, scanty resource, thinnness of tone, couldn't surely put on such manifest power'.[17]

Somehow they do. How are the effects of Narayan's non-literary, storytelling style achieved and how did he come to write in that way?

One answer to the last question may be that he was in reaction against the English style of his father. R. V. Krishnaswami Iyer was a great admirer of the eminent Victorian writers, Macaulay, Carlyle and Pater, and he wrote accordingly. Narayan was sufficiently respectful of the 'literary quality' of his father's style to publish a series of letters he had written to a friend in *Indian Thought*, though for reasons of privacy not disclosing his dead father's identity. Whatever the degree of filial piety involved in the publication, a brief sample from a description of a dream in one of the letters will give an indication of the style Narayan himself sought to avoid:

As softly as sin steals upon the slumbering soul, so came the dusk. Like some vagrant echo from the infinite, wavering and trembling like a timid bird, the dim vision of a soul's desire broke upon his consciousness like a wave far out at sea. The sky was peach purple and the moon was a thread-circle of light, like the marriage-ring of a woman who has long worked for her salty bread. (*Indian Thought*, 239–40)

Peach purple indeed. Narayan, author of early prose rhapsodies with titles like 'Divine Music' may have written like this, but from the time he finished his first novel he never would again. His principle, rather, as he explained in the 'Postcript' to *Talkative Man*, justifying the shortness of the book, was to exclude anything that might inhibit the flow of the narrative, 'laboured detail and description of dress, deportment, facial features, furniture, food and drinks' (*TM* 121), and to prune back repeatedly in first and second revisions. It is this economy and restraint that wins the praise of Jhumpa Lahiri, herself one of the finest of contemporary short story writers: 'While other writers rely on paragraphs and pages to get their points across, Narayan extracts the full capacity of each sentence, so much so that his stories seem bound by an invisible yet essential mechanism, similar to the metrical and quantitative constraints of poetry'.[18] This spare, pared-back style carries us through the action, most often in the consciousness of a single focus character whose ruminations can include flashbacks and anticipations that unobtrusively support the onward momentum of the story. At the same time, there remains room for a leisurely observation yielding the sense of immersion in a variegated and densely peopled landscape.

A passage from Jane Austen can provide a point of reference here. Narayan has frequently been compared to Austen, generally in superficial, oversimplifying terms that are condescending to both writers: their common concentration on a limited social space, their lack of dramatic action, their gentle humour.[19] The description of Emma looking out at the village street of Highbury, however, may be of use for both its likeness and unlikeness to Narayan's fiction:

> Much could not be hoped from the traffic of even the busiest part of Highbury; – Mr Perry walking hastily by, Mr William Cox letting himself in at the office-door, Mr Cole's carriage horse returning from exercise, or a stray letter-boy on an obstinate mule, were the liveliest objects she could presume to expect; and when her eyes fell only on the butcher with his tray, a tidy old woman travelling homewards from shop with her full basket, two curs quarrelling over a dirty bone, and a string of dawdling children round the baker's little bow-window eyeing the gingerbread, she knew she has no reason to complain, and was amused enough; quite enough still to stand at the door. A mind lively and at ease can do with seeing nothing, and can see nothing that does not answer.[20]

The differences from Narayan are more obvious than the similarities here. The very miscellaneousness of what Emma watches is informed by an underlying order, and composes itself into something like a picturesque genre scene. Narayan's Malgudi is more genuinely anarchic as an observed phenomenon. If it has an Austen counterpart, it is in the atypical disorder of Fanny Price's family home in Portsmouth, where everything is conducted in a 'slow bustle', a disorder created (as in Narayan) by too many people, not enough space or money, a complete lack of the security and dignity of the settled big house.[21] Narayan virtually never creates a 'mind lively and at ease' like that of Emma. His characters have none of the social and moral assurance on which this rests, the position articulated in the very first sentence of *Emma*: 'Emma Wodehouse, handsome, clever, and rich, with a comfortable home and happy disposition, seemed to unite some of the best blessings of existence; and had lived nearly twenty-one years in the world with very little to distress or vex her'.[22] Instead Narayan's people have an insecure identity manifested as a perpetual fretfulness of the ego very different from the confident buoyancy of an Emma. Yet for all the differences of social milieu and its conditioned psychology, the experience of Malgudi does give us much of the pleasure attributed to Emma as she watches the street scene in Highbury. For the mind 'lively and at ease' in Narayan's fiction is Narayan's own, expressed in his chosen storytelling style that allows him and his readers to do with seeing nothing, and to see nothing that does not answer.

119

Conclusion

The publication of *Midnight's Children* in 1981, with its high-octane postmodern style, its mythic underlay and its epic version of the history of modern India, gave Indian fiction a completely new visibility. Nothing could ever be the same again. Since then, Rushdie's example has been followed by writers using mythic parallels (Shashi Tharoor's 1989 *The Great Indian Novel*) or dramatizing the impact of contemporary politics (Rohinton Mistry's 1995 *A Fine Balance*). The latest fashion in the twenty-first century seems to be to concentrate on the milieu of the rural peasant, the outcaste and the urban underworld, a sort of 'In Yer Face' India of violence, deprivation and oppression. The nature of this work has varied from Kiran Desai's sombre and serious Booker Prizewinner *The Inheritance of Loss* (2006) through Vikram Chandran's sensational *Sacred Games* (2006) to Aravind Adiga's more obvious and exploitative *The White Tiger*, winner of the 2008 Man Booker Prize. But it appears to have certain common aims: to move the focus away from the middle-class community which has traditionally been the setting for Indian fiction, to make the readers – inevitably also middle class for the most part – guiltily aware of the neglected millions of India's poor and maltreated, and to offer Western readers an India shockingly different from soft-lensed Orientalist images of the spiritual or erotic Other.

In this context, Narayan's work may appear quaint, old-fashioned, appreciated only for its nostalgia value rather than as living literature. Over the last year and a half of receiving daily Google alerts on Narayan, I have seen a fair number of tributes paid to him by younger writers as an influence on their own development, but the great majority of references have been to the film of *The Guide* or the TV series *Malgudi Days*. The nostalgia expressed, indeed, was often for the glory days of Doordashan as India's first nationwide TV station when it broadcast the thirty-nine episodes of *Malgudi Days*, and Narayan's old world Malgudi in the televised resurrection of his stories was remembered through that double filter of sentimental haze. At an academic level, of course, Narayan continues to be more respectfully treated, figuring on almost all university courses on Indian fiction in English, but the tendency is to relegate him to the damaging and deadening position of period classic. An Indian postage stamp issued in 2009 to commemorate Narayan may be taken as symptomatic of his position as distantly revered national icon.

It is difficult to rescue Narayan from this sort of reputation: known, canonized, even read – the 2008 issue of *The Guide* is the sixty-sixth Indian reprint of the book – but with a patronizing lack of understanding. Such has been one of the aims of this study, to try to make clear the sources of Narayan's continuing strength and significance in the post-Rushdie era. In this it is Narayan's imaginative authority that is outstanding. The temptation for the fiction writer, working in a desperately competitive market, is to write reactively to surprise, shock, appease or woo readers by his/her verbal pyrotechnics, unusual subject matter or originality of storytelling. In this regard Narayan's achievement in creating his own imaginative space of Malgudi has still to be seen as quite extraordinary. For someone with his background, a Tamil-speaking Brahmin from South India with limited educational opportunities and no literary connections in the wider English-speaking world, to find the confidence in his own local material and his own voice in English, and to find it in his twenties, remains a kind of miracle.

His persistence with that imaginative territory once found has been viewed as a limitation. Malgudi is a comic place apart, amusing, delightful, dependably the same whatever the vicissitudes of outside phenomenal reality. That sort of ap-preciation has brought an accompanying critique. Narayan is complacent in his lack of attention to Indian society beyond his own South Indian upper caste community, his refusal to deal

121

with the political and social problems of the time. The pattern of so many of his novels where a stranger temporarily disturbs the easy equilibrium of Malgudi day to day life, an equilibrium regained at the novel's end, has been read as the reflection of Narayan's conservative Hindu orthodoxy.

It is important to defend the right of the fiction writer to his or her own imaginative territory, socially restricted though it may be. The depth and resonance of Jane Austen's novels, with their chosen limitations, has long been established. No one faults James Joyce for writing about a very circumscribed community of middle-class Catholic Dubliners as the basis of his fiction, nor yet, to take a more recent Irish example, John McGahern with his career-long mining of the one tiny patch of rural Ireland. The urgencies of India, the sheer scale of injustice, poverty, violence and conflict that afflict it, may lay on the Indian writer a special sense of burdened responsibility. It is out of such a sense that Kiran Desai or Aravind Adiga write. It is not, though, the only way. The imaginative autonomy of Narayan's Malgudi, not directly answerable to the immediate actualities of politics and history, has its own sovereign value. What I have tried to show, in fact, is that the microcosm of Malgudi has a politics of power played out through personal and social relationships and that it is not unchangingly impervious to the impact of modernity. Narayan's gift is to render feelingly the individual experience emmeshed in the fabric of a living environment.

Narayan wrote all his life in English; his books were marketed initially in Britain, later also in the United States, directed towards the world readership of English speakers outside India as much as within. But it is again a part of his imaginative authority that he never sought self-consciously to 'represent' India for its exoticism, its difference, the extremities of its social conditions or even its climate. (There is surprisingly little in Narayan's fiction about heat and dust nor yet about the seasonal downpours of the monsoon.) The fact that it is hot, that the streets are always crowded, that marriages must be arranged with the right astrological advice, are registered as features of a lived landscape too familiar to need explicit comment. And so, to a large extent, it is with Hindu religious practice and belief.

Narayan was a strict vegetarian, a devout Hindu who gave a part of every day to prayer and meditation. His personal and family life was governed by the orthodox pieties of his class and background. But what he depicts in the novels is a secular and social place in which religion, though always there or thereabouts, is never in the foreground. There are the pious old aunts, mothers and grandmothers to voice traditional beliefs, but the protagonists of the books are always more or less modernized men at grips with a material (urban) world. Hindu myths and fables are part of the narrative resources on which Narayan can and does draw and they add a dimension to the fiction differentiating it from traditional European realism. Once again, though, it is without the self-consciousness of later Indian writers building their stories, *Ulysses*-like, on concealed mythic structures. Where sacred legend, folk-tale and parable are part of the normal cultural collectivity, no literary knowingness is necessary for a writer to use them or readers to recognize them.

Of course, Narayan is a distinctively Indian writer, conditioned by his upbringing, background and context. He is in fact one of the very few modern Indian writers in English who lived almost all his life in India itself. The insecure hold on personal identity that characterizes so many of Narayan's people may be locally attributable to subaltern subjection, Margayya with his awe before the European dressed bank secretary, or more fundamentally to Hindu ontological uncertainty – Raju the tourist guide involuntarily transformed into a saint, if that is what happens at the end of *The Guide*. The social scene observed in Malgudi, often satirically observed, is distinctively South Indian down to its addiction to coffee, *dosas* and *idlis*. What Narayan gives us with his deceptively simple style is entry to that creative domain, making us free of it as he is free of it. For such imaginative authority and the generous ease of access to its subtle, funny and compellingly authentic vision, we can only be grateful.

Notes

INTRODUCTION

1. 'Well Met in Malgudi', *TLS*, 9 May 1958. At this stage, *TLS* articles and reviews were not signed.
2. K. R. S. Iyengar, *Indian Writing in English* (New Delhi: Sterling, 1994 [1962]), 360. This statement is re-cycled in many later studies of Narayan: see, for instance, Amar Nath Prasad, *Critical Response to R. K. Narayan* (New Delhi: Sarup, 2003), 2.
3. For references to such comparisons, see Thieme 16, 197.
4. M. K. Naik, *The Ironic Vision: a Study of the Fiction of R. K. Narayan* (New Delhi: Sterling, 1983).
5. William Walsh, *R. K. Narayan: a Critical Appreciation* (London: Heinemann, 1982), 169.
6. See, for example, V. Y. Kantak, *Perspectives in Indian Literary Culture* (Delhi: Pencraft, 1996), 201–16.
7. V. S. Naipaul, *India: a Wounded Civilization* (London: Picador, 2002 [1977]), 12.

CHAPTER 1: THE IMAGINATION OF MALGUDI

1. R. K. Narayan, 'First Person', *Frontline*, October 18 1996, quoted by Meena Sodhi, 'R. K. Narayan: His Life into Art: *Swami and Friends, The English Teacher* and *My Days*' in C.N. Srinath (ed.), *R. K. Narayan: an Anthology of Recent Criticism* (Delhi: Pencraft International, 2000), 92.
2. Susan and N. Ram, *Frontline*, October 18 1996, quoted in Srinath, 92–3.
3. Laxman drew a different sketch-map for *Malgudi Days* (1982), a sort of compendium of the scenes in all of the novels.
4. 'Lawley Extension is south and this river is north of the town', Krishnan points out to his wife Susila, who expresses a desire to go to Lawley Extension by way of the Sarayu (*ET* 55).

5. Benedict Anderson, *Imagined Communities* (London and New York: Verso, 2nd ed. 1991).

6. T. S. Satyan, *Alive and Clicking* (Delhi: Penguin, 2005), 222.

7. See R. K. Laxman, *The Tunnel of Time* in *Collected Writings* (Delhi: Penguin, 2000), 264.

8. Two of these appeared in Narayan's short-lived literary journal *Indian Thought*: 'Watchman of the Lake', and (under the pseudonym N. Rajam), 'The Blindman's Eye'.

9. See Antoinette Quinn, *Patrick Kavanagh* (Dublin: Gill & Macmillan, 2001), 312.

10. On the evidence of Greene's editing of Narayan's work, see Thieme 24.

11. Unpublished letter to Narayan, 21 May 1936, quoted in Ram & Ram 175.

12. See Mulk Raj Anand, *Untouchable* (Mysore: Geetha Book House, 1993 [1935]), Dedication.

13. Raja Rao, *Kanthapura* (New Delhi: Oxford University Press, 2nd ed., 1989 [1938]), 1.

14. See Cynthia Vanden Dreisen, '*Swami and Friends*: Chronicle of an Indian Boyhood', in A.L. McLeod (ed.), *R. K. Narayan: Critical Perspectives* (New Delhi: Sterling, 1994), 167 for an argument against this comparison.

15. Louis MacNeice, 'Snow' in *Collected Poems* (London: Faber, 1966), 30.

16. See Laxman, *Collected Writings*, 265.

17. Lakshmi Holmström, *The Novels of R. K. Narayan* (Calcutta: Writers Workshop, 1973), 104.

18. Although this is the view in the novel, Wendy Doniger points out that you could in fact become a *sanyasi* at any stage of life: personal e-mail, 19 September 2009.

19. Hippolyte Taine's magisterial *Histoire de la littérature anglaise* (1864), in its English translation, continued to be used as a standard authority well into the twentieth century.

20. Undated, unpublished essay in the Narayan papers in Boston University, quoted by Geoffrey Kain in Pier Paolo Piciuccio (ed.), *A Companion to Indian Fiction in English* (New Delhi: Atlantic, 2004), 7.

21. On this aspect of the adaptation of the form of the novel to the Indian situation see Meenakshi Mukherjee, *Realism and Reality: The Novel and Society in India* (Delhi: Oxford University Press, 1994), 68–70.

22. In the story 'Seventh House', collected in *A Horse and Two Goats* (1970), also closely based on Narayan's own experience, the

catastrophic consequence of defying the astrologer's prediction is spelled out.

23. By contrast, two of Narayan's most important interpreters, Thieme himself, and William Walsh, argue for the book's integral success: see Thieme 51–66, and William Walsh, *R. K. Narayan: a Critical Appreciation* (London: Heinemann, 1982), 47–60.

24. C. D. Narasimhaiah, *The Swan and the Eagle* (Shimla: Indian Institute of Advanced Study; Delhi: Motilal Banarsidass, 2nd ed. 1987), 146.

25. Narayan's biographers were given access to the automatic writing of the medium and to a detailed 'psychic journal' kept by the writer, which make clear just how closely the novel is based on his actual experience: see Ram & Ram 262–312, 355–85.

CHAPTER 2: POLITICS AND MARRIAGE

1. Quoted by T. S. Satyan, 'The R. K. Narayan Only I Knew', http://churumuri.wordpress.com/2006/10/10/ts-satyan-the-rk-narayan-only-knew accessed 30 December 2008.

2. T. S. Satyan, personal interview, 8 December 2008.

3. Quoted by Wyatt Mason, 'The Master of Malgudi', *The New Yorker*, 18 December 2006, 86.

4. See, for example, 'Fifteen Years' and 'To a Hindi Enthusiast', (*Nightmare* 14–16, 26–8)

5. An early review of the book already made the comparison with Ibsen: see Ram & Ram, 208.

6. William Walsh, *R. K. Narayan: a Critical Appreciation* (London: Heinemann, 1982) 80.

7. V. S. Naipaul, *India: a Wounded Civilization* (London: Picador, 2002 [1977]), 9.

8. In an illuminating reading of the novel, Richard Cronin comments, '*Waiting for the Mahatma* is a weird hybrid, at once a comic *bildungsroman* and a religious fable of national origin': *Imagining India* (New York: St Martin's Press, 1989), 62.

9. Satish C. Aikant, 'Colonial Ambivalence in R. K. Narayan's *Waiting for the Mahatma*', *Journal of Commonwealth Literature*, 42.2 (June 2007), 89–100.

10. 'Making a Map of the Imagination', R. K. Narayan interviewed by Clare Colvin, *Sunday Times*, 23 April 1989, G9, quoted in Thieme 136.

11. Syd Harrex, 'R. K. Narayan: Painter of Signs', in Srinath, *R. K. Narayan: an Anthology of Recent Criticism*, 75.

12. Lakshmi Holmström, 'Women as Markers of Social Change: *The Dark Room*, *The Guide* and *The Painter of Signs*', in Srinath, 113.

CHAPTER 3: EMBEDDED MYTHS

1. Homi Bhabha, 'A Brahmin in the Bazaar', *TLS*, 8 April 1977, 421.
2. Meenakshi Mukherjee, *The Twice Born Fiction: Themes and Techniques in the Indian Novel in English* (New Delhi and London: Heinemann, 1971), 136.
3. Ibid.
4. The real-life original of the character was nicknamed 'Dhur Margayya – 'One Who Shows the Way to Evil' (*FE*, Introduction). This Introduction, from the original 1952 edition of the novel, is included in the Vintage but not the Indian Thought text of the novel.
5. Fakrul Alam, 'Narrative Strategies in Two Narayan Novels', in A. L. McLeod (ed.), *R. K. Narayan: Critical Perspectives* (New Delhi: Sterling, 1994), 8–21 [10].
6. See, for example, Chitra Sankaram, *Myth Connections: The Use of Hindu Myths and Philosophies in R. K. Narayan and Raja Rao* (Bern: Peter Lang, 2nd ed. 2007 [1995]), Patrick Swinden, 'Hindu Mythology in R. K. Narayan's *The Guide*', *Journal of Commonwealth Literature*, 34.1 (1999), 65–83, and Makarand Panjarape, '"The Reluctant Guru": R. K. Narayan and *The Guide*', *South Asian Review*, 24.2 (2003), 170–86.
7. Sankaram, *Myth Connections*, 245.
8. Panjarape, 'Reluctant Guru', citing Sri Ramakrishna, *Tales and Parables of Sri Ramakrishna* (Madras: Sri Ramakrishna Math, 1989), 144–7.
9. Philip Larkin, 'Church Going', in *Collected Poems* (London: Faber, 1988), 98.
10. Teresa Hubel, 'Devadasi Defiance and *The Man-Eater of Malgudi*', *Journal of Commonwealth Literature*, 29.1 (1994), 15–28. Somewhat strangely, in this article focused on the figure of Rangi in *Man-Eater*, Hubel does not deal with Rosie at all.
11. Sankaram shows that there is a precedent for this form of double narrative in the Hindu form of the tale or *katha*, and in one case in the *Katha Sarit Sagara*, as in *The Guide*, the inset story must be completed before the main frame tale can come to its conclusion: *Myth Connections*, 237.
12. George Orwell, *Shooting an Elephant* (London: Penguin, 2003).
13. Tabish Khair, *Babu Fictions: Alienation in Contemporary Indian Novels* (New Delhi: Oxford University Press, 2001), 234.

14. Richard Cronin, *Imagining India* (New York: St Martin's Press, 1989), 29.
15. Edwin Gerow, 'The Quintessential Narayan', *Literature East and West*, 10.1–2 (1966), 1–18 [12].
16. John Thieme, 'Irony in Narayan's "The Man-Eater of Malgudi"', *The English Review*, 3.4 (1993), 13–17 [16].
17. Ashok Bery, '"Changing the Script": R. K. Narayan and Hinduism', *ARIEL: a Review of International English Literature*, 28.2 (1997), 7–20 [16].

CHAPTER 4: MALGUDI AND MODERNITY

1. Ved Mehta, 'The Train Had Just Arrived at Malgudi Station', in *John Is Easy to Please* (London: Secker & Warburg, 1971), 143.
2. Ibid, 137.
3. Ibid, 139.
4. V. S. Naipaul, *India: a Wounded Civilization* (London: Picador, 2001 [1977]), 17.
5. Ibid, 15.
6. Ibid, 32.
7. See, for example, Ranga Rao, 'Naipaul's Nobel Poise?', *Indian Literature*, 47 (2003), 199–210, though Rao notes a change in attitude in Naipaul's Nobel address in which Narayan is the only Indian writer cited.
8. Naipaul, 12.
9. See, for example, Makarand Panjarape, '"The Reluctant Guru": R. K. Narayan and *The Guide*', *South Asian Review*, 24.2 (2003), 170–86. For a similar stress on Narayan's Hindu orthodoxy, see Michael Gorra, 'History, Maya, Dharma: the Novels of R. K. Narayan' in A.L. McLeod, *R. K. Narayan: Critical Perspectives* (New Delhi: Sterling, 1994), 42–52.
10. Sudesh Mishra, 'R. K. Narayan: The Malgudisation of Reality', in McLeod, 86–95 [87].
11. Naipaul, 15.
12. William Walsh, *R. K. Narayan: a Critical Appreciation* (London: Heinemann, 1982), 62–3.
13. See http://www.upperstall.com/films/1952/mr-sampat, accessed 23 July 2009.
14. Naipaul, 15.
15. Interview with William Walsh, BBC Third Programme, 22 February 1968, quoted in M. K. Naik, *The Ironic Vision: a Study of the Fiction of R. K. Narayan* (New Delhi: Sterling, 1983), 21.

16. Letter to R. K. Narayan, 15 March 1966 in Graham Greene, *A Life in Letters*, ed. Richard Greene (London: Little Brown, 2007), 282–3.
17. There are minor textual differences between the Indian and the British editions of *The Vendor of Sweets*: I have followed the Indian text throughout.
18. Naipaul, 32.
19. Ibid, 33.

CHAPTER 5: STORYTELLING STYLES

1. All three of these stories were first collected in *A Horse and Two Goats* (1970) and are included in *Under the Banyan Tree* (1985).
2. The story, originally published as 'End of the World' in *The Hindu* in 1938, was collected in *Cyclone, and Other Stories* (1944) and again in *Lawley Road* (1956): see Ram & Ram 421.
3. *Meet Mr Mulliner* (1927) was the first in a series of collections of short stories by Wodehouse that featured Mulliner as storyteller.
4. 'The Tiger's Claw', 'The Snake-Song' and 'Lawley Road' are collected in *Malgudi Days* (1982), 'The Roman Image' and 'A Career' in *Under the Banyan Tree* (1985). Somewhat confusingly *Malgudi Days* was the title Narayan gave to his first 1943 collection of stories as well as the 1982 selection and the popular Hindi TV series of the 1980s; all three have different contents from one another.
5. There is in fact a Sanskrit source story for *All's Well that End's Well*, and the motif is widespread in India: Wendy Doniger, personal e-mail, 19 September 2009.
6. This is the view of John Hawley in '''R. K. Narayanswami B.A.B.L. Engine Driver'': Story-telling and Memory in *The Grandmother's Tale, and Selected Stories*', *South Asian Review*, 23.1 (2002), 86–105, cited in Thieme 183, 228.
7. See Krishna Sen, 'With the real Dr Rann please stand up?', *South Asian Review*, 23.1 (2002), 22–48.
8. John Thieme (157) cites *The South Bank Show*, London Weekend Television, 1983, as the source for the identification of Garfield, taken by Narayan as a tiger.
9. As Walter Goodman put it, in an otherwise positive review of the novel, the Master's 'miracles come a touch easy and his philosophy and imagery are right out of the Mystical East mango patch', *New York Times*, 8 August 1983.
10. The famous Tamil writer Kalki, for example, in his Foreword to the Tamil translation of *Swami and Friends* in 1940, urged Narayan for the future to 'write in his native tongue': see Ram & Ram 318.

11. Raja Rao, *Kanthapura* (New Delhi: Oxford University Press, 2nd ed., 1989), v.

12. In his very first letter to Narayan, Greene, after expressing his admiration for the manuscript of *Swami and Friends*, asked 'Have you any objection to a few alterations in the English? It's very good on the whole, but at times the grammar and sense need tightening'. Graham Greene, *A Life in Letters*, ed. Richard Greene (London: Little Brown, 2007), 69. Narayan gratefully accepted and Greene in fact worked on all of the novels before publication up to *The Man-Eater of Malgudi*, on which he commented to the publisher, 'Narayan needs a good deal of editing to make his English smooth enough without destroying the Indian quality but I always do this myself': unpublished letter to A. S. Frere of Heinemann, quoted by Thieme 199.

13. A recent extreme example is Vikram Chandra's epic Mumbai underworld novel *Sacred Games* (London: Faber, 2006), for which a huge multilingual glossary has been made available on the author's website: http://www.vikramchandra.com/Default.aspx ?tabid=157.

14. See, for example, *Waiting for the Mahatma* and *The World of Nagaraj* in both Western and Indian editions.

15. Ved Mehta, *John is Easy to Please* (London: Secker and Warburg, 1971), 149.

16. Shashi Tharoor, 'R. K. Narayan's Comedies of Suffering', in *Bookless in Baghdad* (New Delhi: Penguin Viking, 2005), 84.

17. V. Y. Kantak, *Perspectives on Indian Literary Fiction* (Delhi: Pencraft, 1996), 21.

18. Jhumpa Lahiri, Foreword to a re-issue of *Malgudi Days*, quoted by Wyatt Mason, 'The Master of Malgudi', *The New Yorker*, 18 December, 2006, 86.

19. See Tharoor, *Bookless in Baghdad*, 83–4 for a relatively recent example of this comparison, well-established in older criticism.

20. Jane Austen, *Emma*, ed. Richard Cronin and Dorothy McMillan (Cambridge: Cambridge University Press, 2005), 251.

21. Jane Austen, *Mansfield Park*, ed. Kathryn Sutherland (London: Penguin, 1996), 361.

22. Austen, *Emma*, 3.

Bibliography

WORKS BY R. K. NARAYAN

Swami and Friends (London: Hamish Hamilton, 1935)
The Bachelor of Arts (London: Nelson, 1937)
The Dark Room (London: Macmillan, 1938)
The English Teacher (London: Eyre and Spottiswoode, 1945)
Mr Sampath – the Printer of Malgudi (London: Eyre and Spottiswoode, 1949)
The Financial Expert (London: Methuen, 1952)
Waiting for the Mahatma (London: Methuen, 1955)
The Guide (London: Methuen, 1958)
The Man-Eater of Malgudi (London: Heinemann, 1961)
Gods, Demons and Others (New York: Viking, 1964)
My Dateless Diary: An American Journey (Mysore: Indian Thought Publications, 1964)
The Vendor of Sweets (London: Bodley Head, 1967)
A Horse and Two Goats (New York: Viking, 1970)
The Ramayana: a Shortened Modern Prose Version of the Indian Epic (New York: Viking, 1972)
My Days: a Memoir (New York: Viking, 1974)
The Painter of Signs (New York: Viking, 1976)
The Mahabharata: a Shortened Modern Prose Version of the Indian Epic (New York: Viking, 1978)
Malgudi Days (London: Heinemann, 1982)
A Tiger for Malgudi (London: Heinemann, 1983)
Under the Banyan Tree and Other Stories (London: Heinemann, 1985)
Talkative Man (London: Heinemann, 1986)
A Writer's Nightmare (New Delhi: Penguin, 1988)
The World of Nagaraj (London: Heinemann, 1990)
Grandmother's Tale (Chennai: Indian Thought Publications, 1992)
The Grandmother's Tale: Three Novellas (London: Heinemann, 1993)

Indian Thought: a Miscellany (New Delhi: Penguin, 1997)
The Writerly Life, ed. S. Krishnan (New Delhi: Penguin, 2001)

BIOGRAPHY

Ram, Susan and N. Ram, *R. K. Narayan: the Early Years 1906–1945* (New Delhi: Viking Penguin, 1996).

CRITICAL STUDIES

This includes works that contain essays on or references to Narayan.

Aikant, Satish C., 'Colonial Ambivalence in R. K. Narayan's *Waiting for the Mahatma*', *Journal of Commonwealth Literature*, 42.2 (June 2007), 89–100.

Bery, Ashok, '"Changing the Script": R. K. Narayan and Hinduism', *ARIEL: a Review of International English Literature*, 28.2 (1997), 7–20.

Bhabha, Homi, 'A Brahmin in the Bazaar', *TLS*, 8 April 1977.

Cronin, Richard, *Imagining India* (New York: St Martin's Press, 1989).

Gerow, Edwin, 'The Quintessential Narayan', *Literature East and West*, 10.1–2 (1966), 1–18.

Holmström, Lakshmi, *The Novels of R. K. Narayan* (Calcutta: Writers Workshop, 1973).

Hubel, Teresa, 'Devadasi Defiance and *The Man-Eater of Malgudi*', *Journal of Commonwealth Literature*, 29.1 (1994), 15–28.

Iyengar, K. R. S., *Indian Writing in English* (New Delhi: Sterling, 1994 [1962]).

Kantak, V.Y., *Perspectives in Indian Literary Culture* (Delhi: Pencraft, 1996).

Khair, Tabish, *Babu Fictions: Alienation in Contemporary Indian Novels* (New Delhi: Oxford University Press, 2001).

McLeod, A. L. (ed.), *R. K. Narayan: Critical Perspectives* (New Delhi: Sterling, 1994).

Mason, Wyatt, 'The Master of Malgudi', *The New Yorker*, 18 December 2006.

Mehta, Ved, *John Is Easy to Please* (London: Secker & Warburg, 1971).

Mukherjee, Meenakshi, *The Twice Born Fiction: Themes and Techniques in the Indian Novel in English* (New Delhi and London: Heineman, 1971).

Naik, M. K., *The Ironic Vision: a Study of the Fiction of R. K. Narayan* (New Delhi: Sterling, 1983).

Naipaul, V. S., *India: a Wounded Civilization* (London: Picador, 2002 [1977]).

Narasimhaiah, C. D., *The Swan and the Eagle* (Shimla: Indian Institute of Advanced Study; Delhi: Motilal Banarsidass, 2nd ed. 1987).

Panjarape, Makarand, '"The Reluctant Guru"': R. K. Narayan and *The Guide'*, *South Asian Review*, 24.2 (2003), 170–86.

Piciuccio, Pier Paolo (ed.), *A Companion to Indian Fiction in English* (New Delhi: Atlantic, 2004).

Rao, Ranga, 'Naipaul's Nobel Poise?', *Indian Literature*, 47 (2003), 199–210.

Sankaram, Chitra, *Myth Connections: The Use of Hindu Myths and Philosophies in R. K. Narayan and Raja Rao* (Bern: Peter Lang, 2nd ed. 2007 [1995]).

Sen, Krishna, 'With the real Dr Rann please stand up?', *South Asian Review*, 23.1 (2002), 22–48.

Srinath, C. N. (ed.), *R. K. Narayan: an Anthology of Recent Criticism* (Delhi: Pencraft International, 2000).

Swinden, Patrick, 'Hindu Mythology in R. K. Narayan's *The Guide'*, *Journal of Commonwealth Literature*, 34.1 (1999), 65–83.

Thieme, John, *R. K. Narayan* (Manchester: Manchester University Press, 2007).

——, 'Irony in Narayan's "The Man-Eater of Malgudi"', *The English Review*, 3.4 (1993), 13–17.

Walsh, William, *R. K. Narayan: a Critical Appreciation* (London: Heinemann, 1982).

RELATED MATERIALS

Anand, Mulk Raj, *Untouchable* (Mysore: Geetha Book House, 1993 [1935]).

Anderson, Benedict, *Imagined Communities* (London and New York: Verso, 2nd ed. 1991).

Greene, Graham, *A Life in Letters*, ed. Richard Greene (London: Little Brown, 2007).

Laxman, R. K., *Collected Writings* (Delhi: Penguin, 2000).

Mukherjee, Meenakshi, *Realism and Reality: The Novel and Society in India* (Delhi: Oxford University Press, 1994).

Quinn, Antoinette, *Patrick Kavanagh* (Dublin: Gill & Macmillan, 2001).

Rao, Raja, *Kanthapura* (New Delhi: Oxford University Press, 2nd ed., 1989 [1938]).

Satyan, T. S., *Alive and Clicking* (Delhi: Penguin, 2005).

Index

Figures in bold indicate the sections where individual works are discussed in detail.

Adiga, Aravind 45, 120, 122
  Between the Assassinations 45
  White Tiger 120
Allahabad 110
American Mercury 10
Anand, Mulk Raj 2, 11, 44, 116
  Untouchable 11, 44
Anand, Vijay 64
Anderson, Benedict 7
Aquinas, St Thomas 22
Atlantic 10
Austen, Jane 2, 23–4, 118, 122
  Emma 118, 119
  Mansfield Park 118

Bellow, Saul 1, 79, 80, 81
  The Victim 79, 80–1
Bery, Ashok 78
Bhabha, Homi 56
Bhagavad-Gita 60, 94
Bhose, Subhas Chandra 48
Birla House 48
Bookman 10
Brontë, Charlotte
  Jane Eyre 19
Browning, Robert 9
Byron, Lord 9, 22

Carlyle, Thomas 117
Chamarajapuram 7
Chandra, Vikhram 120
  Sacred Games 120

Chekhov, A.P. 1, 103, 104
Cheluviengar, M.S. 86
Chennapatna 8, 9
Coimbatore 6, 23, 84
Congress Party 73
Corelli, Marie 9
Crompton, Richmal 13
Cronin, Richard 76

Danielewski, Ted 64
Delhi 7
Desai, Kiran 120
  The Inheritance of Loss 120
Dickens, Charles 9
  David Copperfield 18, 27
Dublin 8

Faulkner, William 2, 89, 116
Fitzgerald, F. Scott 89
Foucault, Michel 3
Forster, E.M. 1, 11

Gandhi, Indira 45, 50, 51, 84
Gandhi, M.K. 11, 44, 45, 49, 50, 74, 95, 96
Gandhi, Rahjiv 45
Gandhi, Sanjay 50, 52
Gerow, Edwin 77, 78
Greene, Graham 1, 10, 13, 72, 79, 80, 93, 103, 116
  The End of the Affair 79, 80

Haggard, H. Rider 9
Hamilton, Hamish 10, 13
Hardy, Thomas 2, 9
Harper's 10
Heaney, Seamus 10
Hemingway, Ernest 116
Hindi 36
Hindu 36, 84, 103
Holmström, Lakshmi 20, 55
Hubel, Teresa 68

Ibsen, Henrik 38
Doll's House 38, 39, 42
Iyengar, K.R.S. 2

Joyce, James 8, 19, 104, 122
Portrait of the Artist as a Young Man 18, 19, 22
Ulysses 57
Justice 19, 36

Kannada 6, 9, 11, 116
Kantak, V.Y. 116
Karnataka 6
Kavanagh, Patrick 10
Keats, John 9
Kennedy, J.F. 94
Khair, Tabish 72
Kipling, Rudyard 13
Stalky & Co 13
Krishnaswami Iyer, R.V. 117
Kukanahalli Tank 9
Kumbakonan 6
Kumbh Mela 110, 111

Lahiri, Jhumpa 117
Lalgudi 6
Lawrence, D.H. 19, 45, 104
Sons and Lovers 18, 19
Laxman, R.K. 6, 9, 36

Macaulay, T.B. 117
McGahern, John 122
MacNeice, Louis 16
Madras 6, 8, 15, 19, 36, 68, 84, 103
Madras, Presidency 6
Maharaja's College, University of Mysore 6, 18, 35

Maharaja's Collegiate School 9, 18
Manchester Guardian 10
Mangudi 6
Mansfield, Katherine 104
Marlowe, Christopher 9
Mehta, Ved 83
Mistry, Rohinton 50, 120
Fine Balance 50
Molière, J.-B. P. 9
Mukherjee, Meenakshi 57
Twice Born Fiction 57
Mysore 6, 7, 8, 9, 19, 33, 35, 36, 84, 103

Naipaul, V.S. 1, 2, 35, 46, 78, 84, 85, 88, 91
India: a Wounded Civilization 78, 84, 91
Narasimhaiah, C.D. 29
Narayan, Hema 33, 87
Narayan, Rajam 28, 87
Narayan, R.K.
Astrologer's Day and Other Stories 103
Bachelor of Arts 3, 5, 15, 17, 18, 19, 21, **22–7**, 28, 37, 42, 44, 45, 86, 98
Dark Room 3, **37–43**, 55, 56 , 99
English Teacher 3, 5, 17, 19, 21, 22, **27–34**, 109
Financial Expert 3, **58–63**, 68, 93
Gods, Demons and Others 56–7, 58, 102
'Grandmother's Tale' 4, **106–9**
Guide 1, 3, 5, 25, 29, 55, 58, **63–72**, 73, 75, 77, 79, 80, 81, 89, 109, 110, 112, 121, 123
Indian Thought 85, 86, 117
Mahabharata 56, 58, 102
Malgudi Days 83, 103, 106, 121
Man-Eater of Malgudi 3, 58, 63, 64, **72–8**, 79, 81, 109
Mr Sampath, Printer of Malgudi 4, 57, 84, **85–93**, 97, 100
My Dateless Diary 72, 83
My Days 8, 9, 10, 12, 19, 23, 28–9, 33, 36, 37, 43, 86, 94, 106
Painter of Signs 3, 36, **50–5**, 56, 57, 94, 107

Ramayana 57, 58, 60, 73, 94, 102
Swami and Friends 3, 5, 10, **11–17**, 20, 21, 27, 28, 37, 43, 44, 87
Talkative Man 4, 105, 109, 117
Tiger for Malgudi 4, **110–15**
Under the Banyan Tree 44
Vendor of Sweets 4, 84, 85, **93–101**, 110, 115
Waiting for the Mahatma 3, 6, 16, 29, 36, **45–50**, 51, 53, 94
World of Nagaraj 5, 100, 104
Writerly Life 51, 84
Writer's Nightmare 7, 64, 71, 97, 110
Nehru, Jawaharlal 74
New York 83
New Yorker 83
New York Review of Books 84

Orwell, George 70
'Shooting an Elephant' 70

Panjarape, Makarand 64
Pater, Walter 22, 117
Pope, Alexander 9
Prasad, H.Y.S. 35
Punch 87
Purnu, Kittu 10, 103

Rajya Sabha 35
Ram, N. 6, 86, 89, 103, 105
Ram, Susan 6, 86, 89, 103, 105
Ramakrishna, Sri 64, 72
Rao, Raja 2, 44, 116
Kanthapura 11, 12, 44, 45, 116
Rushdie, Salman 116, 120
Midnight's Children 45, 50, 57, 120

Sahitya Akademi 1, 63, 64
Sankaram, Chitaram 64

Sanskrit 94, 102
Satyan, T.S. 9, 35
Shakespeare, William 108
All's Well that Ends Well 108
Cymbeline 108
Shaw, G.B. 39
Mrs Warren's Profession 39
Shelley, P.B. 9
Singh, Kushwant 45
Train to Pakistan 45
Squire, J.C. 10
Srinivas, R.K. 9
Srinivasan, T.S. 89, 90
Stein, Gertrude 116
Strand Magazine 10

Taine, H. 21
History of English Literature 21
Tamil Nadu 6
Tamil 6, 8, 9, 115
Tate, Maurice 13, 16
Tharoor, Shashi 116, 120
The Great Indian Novel 120
Thieme, John 3, 13, 28, 51, 57, 70, 77, 78
Time 35
Times Literary Supplement 1
Times of India 36
Tolstoy, L.N. 9
Childhood, Boyhood, Youth 18
Trichy (Tiruchirapalli) 6
Trollope, Anthony 5

United Services College 13
Updike, John 1

Walsh, William 45
Wodehouse, P.G. 17, 106
Wodeyar rajas 6, 9

Lightning Source UK Ltd.
Milton Keynes UK
UKHW020212031118
331668UK00003B/37/P